1

Table of Contents

Prologue
My Story: Justin Spears

The year was 2005. I had spent the last four years of my life working various sales jobs. At the time I was working as a sales rep for a document destruction company in Cincinnati, OH. It was a cutthroat, outside sales position with very little client relations work. Everything was driven by "activity". This was a buzzword that consisted of telemarketing, cold calling, setting sales appointments and closing sales calls. Nothing mattered other than hitting targets. It was a "what have you done for me lately" environment. After about a year of banging away at simply hitting numbers, I had become a monster. I hated every moment of what I was doing. It was only my wife and I at the time. She was in graduate school studying to be a speech language pathologist. As she approached graduation, we both decided it would be best to move back home. Home is central Indiana where we both grew up and met in high school. A new start, with a blank slate awaited us. As this transition occurred, I decided it was time for another transition; a career change.

I made the decision to leave the sales world. I graduated from Butler University in 2001 with a degree in Marketing. "*We are the Harvard of the Midwest*". This mantra was repeated all over campus during my time at Butler and while I am not naive enough to believe that simply having a degree would guarantee any job I wanted, we were certainly sold on the power of a Butler degree. Instead of landing the cushy account executive position, with a company car, cell phone and expense account, I found myself stocking produce at a local grocery store. From there I found jobs that were closer to what I had imagined as I was sitting in the classroom listening to professors explain what we needed to know as we moved toward the "real world". As I was going through this phase, I remember asking myself "how did I get here?"

As I walked on to campus in 1997 I entered as a history major. I went to Butler for two reasons. First, I was told I was going to college; no ifs, and or buts. It was the golden ticket to assure that I would stay out of poverty. Second, my mom had taken a position at the university while I was in high school. Prior to that, I wanted to attend Purdue University and study Meteorology. With my mom's position at Butler, I would receive free tuition. It was a no brainer. I would live at home to save even more money. The only obstacle; admittance.

I was not a strong academic student in high school. I was bored and disengaged. I did enough to get by. I was never a troublemaker, I just did not have any interest in what school had to offer. The only subject I found remotely interesting was history. I graduated with a 2.7 G.P.A and my SAT and ACT scores were average at best. Needless to say, I would not have been a target for a school like Butler. My mom was able to arrange a meeting with an admissions counselor and I was able to sell them enough on my desire to succeed, along with my strong Senior year in high school. It was enough to get me admitted on academic probation. I spent one semester as a history major before switching to the School of Business. I switched due to needing a foreign language requirement that I did not think I could meet; along with coming to the realization that the job prospects for a history major looked bleak. If anything, I would have taught.

Fast forward back to 2005, as I settled in at home I made a decision to give the teaching option a try. I entered a Transition to Teaching program for working adults. This was an accelerated two year program. I spent the first year completing undergraduate social studies courses, including; history, geography and U.S. government. The second year was focused on education.

After completing my student teaching in the summer of 2007, I was ready to enter the classroom. As the often quipped Yankee catcher Yogi Berra once said; "It was deja vu all over again." I remember professors yammering on about the job prospects for male social studies teachers, especially for those who were willing to coach. After filling out applications with 12 different school districts, I got exactly zero job offers. What was I going to do? I waited for the school year to start and I scanned the job boards one last time to see if any positions remained unfilled. I came across a business position that was open in a rural district. I interviewed and subsequently got the position. My teaching career was off and running.

Why did I become a teacher? I've been asked this question numerous times. I have always had an affinity for working with people and more importantly feeling like I am helping someone along their path in life. Even in my days as a sales rep, I enjoyed meeting needs with a solution. Sometimes that was a difficult process, but I always felt satisfaction out of those situations. I wanted to bring my experience of working in the business world to the classroom. I didn't want to fill students' brains with book knowledge. Instead, I wanted to share my thoughts and experiences as they transitioned into the next phase of their life. I wanted to prepare them, no matter what route they would take after leaving high school. I felt I could make a difference.

There it is. That tried and true saying that so many educators rest their hat on; making a difference. I remember before the era of the meme, there was a chain email going around about a teacher that was attending a party and the attendees were all going around telling each other how much money they made the previous year. When they got to the teacher the others are throwing jabs at how little the *teacher* must make. The person goes on a diatribe about how important the role of teacher is and ends with the haymaker; "I make a difference!"

Over my 10 years in the classroom I have come to understand this story is fraudulent. During this time my eyes have been opened to the vile and sinister nature of compulsory schooling. I am writing this book to share my thoughts and experiences as to why this is true. I have seen firsthand how much this system of mass, forced schooling is failing our youth, families and ultimately communities. Day after day, year after year, students shuffle in to schools under the false pretenses of being educated. Instead, they are wasting away their one and only shot at being educated. Their most fruitful and productive years are spent in buildings that resemble prisons. Their desire and curiosity to learn is being replaced by breaking their spirits and drilling them with useless facts. The system is an unmitigated failure.

I want to be clear. I make no point to attack the people in public schooling. Afterall, I am a part of the machine. What I intend to accomplish with this book is to tell the story of a system; an American schooling system that is corrupt in its founding and has in many ways accomplished what it was set out to do. We know there are parents out there that are questioning what is going on in schools. We know there are parents thirsting for options to the local public school. This book may lead to more questions and hopefully provide some inspiration and solutions for the reader.

I hope to open your eyes to the failure of schooling. In arriving at the title of this book someone told me "It (schooling) is not a failure, it has accomplished exactly what it was designed to do!" This still does not diminish the fact that we must call out this system for what it is; an unmitigated disaster. I will attempt to tell you the story and evolution of schooling in America. In addition, I will rely on my near decade of experience in the classroom to highlight how the foundation and evolution has grown to be so sinister. Finally, I hope to inspire you with a vision. A vision that is not so fuzzy, but crystal clear in its goals and objectives. We can throw off the chains of compulsory schooling and return to a free thinking, self reliant society. It will require a level of engagement by parents and community leaders like we have not seen since colonial days. The only question is; are you up for the challenge?

Part I: The History of the American School System

1. The System

The United States school system has worked well for many in this country: it has secured reliably consistent paychecks for teachers, administrators, support staff, and union leaders. Colleges have enjoyed exploding enrollments and higher-than-ever revenues. Politicians have found a loyal and influential partner in their election campaigns. Vendors have appreciated a dependable client all too willing to spend.

The only problem with the system is that it has not been that great for students. On the hierarchy of who benefits from education policy, students, unfortunately, rank near the bottom. The past fifteen years in a public school classroom has made that fact crystal clear to me, although it was not always.

As an energetic education graduate, I never put any thought into the school system at all. Schools were always just there, with no reason to be analyzed or questioned. The concept of disentangling education from schooling had never occurred to me. I knew education was important, therefore schooling was important. My role as a teacher, I thought, was to prepare kids for the real experiences of an unforgiving world. I was ready: I was going to refuse to coddle them, I was going to challenge them, I wouldn't accept excuses, and I would churn out the type of prepared young adults that our new millennia demanded. In short, I had always focused on what my role would be within the system; the system itself was simply accepted.

Not understanding the system made day-to-day issues in the classroom even more frustrating. Problems would arise but I lacked the context to comprehend them. When the kids would act out behaviorally I never questioned the system, I would question only the kids or my management practices. I'd try the newest pedagogic theory (which would come around every few years or so to revolutionize education) only to realize that it didn't change anything; nor would the third or the fourth thing I tried. When the students were bored with my lesson, I wouldn't question the system, but only the kids, or my lesson. I'd change my lessons to be in line with the next instructional fad but once again the results would mimic those from before. I so badly wanted students to share my passion for history and economics, but one thing remained unchanged: they were bored and they didn't want to be there. They were no different than I was at that age and no different than the generation before that. It would take over a decade of this constant frustration, combined with curiosity, and some serious scrutiny, before considering that it wasn't necessarily me boring them, but the system.

The school system was originally created to reinforce obedience to the state. It was imported from Germany in the 19th century, who installed it to mold kids into acquiescent nationalists. Later on, nativist American politicians saw it as a useful tool in dealing with throngs of not-so-Protestant immigrants. As it matured, its employees saw opportunities to secure reliably consistent, taxpayer-funded salaries. The appeal of exemption from market forces brought about action to replace a largely private system of education with a mandatory public system. These changes were certainly not initiated by students, nor by parents unhappy with the existing education arrangements. The shift to compulsory taxpayer-funded schooling provided a mutually beneficial opportunity to both politicians and education employees. One would enjoy financial security, the other political security.

With the arrangement working for both, the system grew. Nonexistent for the first 200 years of our nation's history, our public school system now employs more than six million people nationwide. That's more than the top 10 private employers in the US, *combined*. In fact, since 1950, public school employees have grown at a rate four times faster than the student body.

System employees have also managed to enjoy some perks unheard of in the private economy. The system has succeeded in guaranteeing more employees and larger salaries, even in areas where there are fewer students and poorer performances. No private enterprise could exist as such (but politicians can simply issue exemptions from pesky market nuisances). For instance, a recent study by Benjamin Scafidi shows that between 1992-2009, while the number of students in DC Public Schools decreased by 15%, the number of administrators and non-teaching personnel increased by 42%. This is not unique to DC either. The study shows that if staffing across the United States had increased at the same rate as student populations, there would be over 600,000 fewer administrative or non-teaching jobs.

Of course none of these staffing increases are linked to performance; a Department of Education study in 2009 showed DC Public Schools finished dead last in the nation for 4th grade reading proficiency, yet they led the nation in adjusted per pupil spending. That year their teachers were also bringing in the 6th highest average salaries. As for the students: more than half of the district's fourth graders scored "below basic" when it came to reading proficiency.

Despite what you may see on the news (such as eight year olds holding signs and robotically chanting), proposals to change the system are never spurned by students, only its beneficiaries. The vast majority of students hate school and would welcome *any* type of change, but the system is not about students. Critics of reform tell us that the school system is indispensable, but these are usually people either politically or financially dependent on it. Their answers to simple questions rarely amount to more than shallow or emotional platitudes. Questions such as: why do students need to take so many different subjects? How does hour-long instruction in five to six subjects a day improve retention? Why does the state choose which classes kids must take rather than families? Where is the evidence to show minimum requirements on days per year improve outcomes? How has standardized testing made kids smarter? Why do all teenagers need to learn algebra? Why does the state issue graduation waivers to teenagers who haven't learned algebra, if all teenagers need to learn algebra? Have mandatory P.E. and Health classes reduced obesity rates over time? Do mandatory Government and Economics classes increase civic literacy? There are certainly many more, but you get the point: longer school days, longer school years, more subjects, and mandatory subjects, all benefit staff far more than students.

Believe it or not, there was a time in this country's history where education was left mainly up to the family or local community. Most Americans understood the value of education and didn't require government threats to improve their lives. Nor was this a socially, politically, or economically stagnant period. One of the most vibrant, robust, active time periods in our nation's history took place with virtually no government mandated schooling.

2. Early America: Education without mandates

If we are to accept the critic's claims that mandatory schooling is essential for mass education, then this should be the easiest thing in the world to prove. We simply go back to a time when there was no compulsory schooling, then observe the social and economic lag which follows. Yet America advanced quite impressively between the early 17th and mid 19th centuries.

One of my favorite examples is the Great Exhibition, an international industrial exhibit which took place in London in 1851. This was just one year before our country's first compulsory education law was enacted (Massachusetts, 1852). At this time Americans were not considered industrial innovators, in fact the country was still viewed as a cultural backwater by many haughty Europeans. At the event, the British press made it a special point to sharply mock the American exhibit. Yet the ingenuity of the American products shocked everyone. Cyrus McCormick's reaper wowed throngs of onlookers, especially when it outperformed a British reaper in a side by side test. Cyrus McCormick received virtually all of his education in his father's barn.

Samuel Colt displayed his innovative Model 1851 Navy at the Exhibition (a quick firing revolver), but then also disassembled and reassembled ten different guns using different parts from each gun. His use of interchangeable parts helped pave the way for the type of assembly line production which came to characterize almost all late 19th and early 20th century manufacturing. Colt was an indentured servant on a farm at age 11, and worked in a textile factory at age 15.

None of this is to suggest a causal relationship, any pro-school advocate could point to all of the current miracles created on the watch of industrialized schooling. It's simply to show that schooling is no prerequisite for economic advancement. That is because across the world and across time, economic freedom has always been the strongest indicator of material progress. Current World Bank data still shows virtually no correlation between duration of compulsory education and economic advancement.

The First American Colonies

In the 17th century, education in the New World varied depending on where you settled. For the most part, education was something that people received in the home, although schools soon became fairly common across the colonies. The big difference is they were locally governed, and basically voluntary.

You probably would have been least likely to attend a school if you lived in the southern colonies. Not necessarily because they didn't want, or value, schools, but because geographic factors limited their feasibility. Larger farms and scattered settlements made schools far less common than they were in the north. Many kids received the education they needed as apprentices. Others who were not apprenticed out might learn literacy skills through their local churches. The SPG[1] was active in the South and set up charity schools to teach religion and literacy. In other cases there were "old field schools," where abandoned buildings in tobacco fields were used to teach basics to local children (this is how George Washington received his early education). There were also fully private schools which charged tuition, and endowed schools which offered discounted tuition thanks to wealthy benefactors who contributed land and money to ensure education regardless of class (slaves, of course, being the exception). The wealthiest families in the south could afford private tutors and of course had no need for schools.

In the middle colonies formal schools would be a bit more common than they were in the South. The tremendous diversity in religion there meant numerous institutions were established to inculcate kids in the appropriate faith. English Protestants, some Calvinists, and Quakers all competed to ensure their doctrine reached as many as possible. Although fees were collected, many of these were accessible to even the poorest families. In Philadelphia we also see one of the

---

[1] *Society for the Propagation of the Gospel in Foreign Parts. It was organized by the Church of England, sending clergymen to all of Britain's colonies worldwide to establish schools and churches.

earliest trends away from classical curricula. In 1750 the Philadelphia Academy offered History, Geography, Foreign Language, Geometry, Surveying, and Navigation, among other subjects. This was a departure from the standard Reading, Writing, Greek, or Latin which characterized many schools of the 17th century. Academies were also set up for girls, teaching sewing, dancing, etiquette, or other subjects deemed appropriate for females at the time. Philadelphia also provided a number of low cost night schools available to apprentices or working adults.

The New England colonies bequeathed free, compulsory government education to this country (more on this in chapter 4), but it took a while before such a system would gain a monopoly over education. As was the case in most of the colonies, most New Englanders learned literacy at home; it was common to know how to read before ever entering school. Outside of the home there were all kinds of arrangements made to ensure literacy of the young. In many towns "dame schools" were common. These were private arrangements which came at a nominal fee. Usually a young, educated woman of the town would host classes out of her home teaching basic skills and literacy. If students were too poor to afford the fee for education, the town might see to it that they attend for free. Similar to the rest of the Atlantic seaboard, New England also had full-tuition private schools, partial-tuition private schools, grammar schools, secondary schools, parochial schools, private tutoring, apprenticeships, and tutoring. Overall, one simple principle guided education in the American colonies: supply and demand.

Colonists wanted to make the most of their freedoms and there existed a steady supply of instruction available to them. The sheer number of bookstores in colonial cities (fifty-plus in both Boston and Philadelphia) could not have existed if the population had not educated itself. While a compulsory system never existed, Jerome Reich observes in his book Colonial America: *"by the time of the Revolution, education was more accessible in the colonies than in any nation of western Europe."* Additionally, in Education and the State, E.G. West concludes: *"schooling in the early nineteenth century was already almost universal without being compulsory."* And in The Birth of America, William Polk notes that: *"Americans tended to be better educated than Europeans of comparable means."* No government mandates, no truancy laws, no minimum hours or minimum days, yet the American colonies remained among the most educated places in the world. Unfortunately, as was often the case, Americans still tended to look to Europe for guidance. There was a certain respect afforded to the continent despite the bloody and costly effort to split from it. And shortly after our independence, even though levels of education were extremely high, Americans looked back across the Atlantic for guidance on a more formal, standard system of schooling.

3. Compulsory Schooling: from Europe to America

The American school system is more of a European import than an American innovation. A century before the first permanent settlers made their way here on the Mayflower, Europe was trying their hand at mandatory government schooling. The Reformation is a good place to begin, as before that, education was largely left to families or the Church. It also makes geographic sense as the earliest roots of our current school system are largely German.

Martin Luther, leader of the Protestant Reformation in Germany, sought out the State to force kids to learn what he wanted them to learn. Schooling was not about education, but rather education in the ways of Lutheranism. For Luther, the old tradition of leaving education to the families was too risky. Much like educational statists today, he simply did not trust families to convey the information he wanted conveyed.

In 1524 Luther writes, referring to proper home education, that the common man "doesn't have the means for it, doesn't want to do it, and doesn't know how." Luther's chief collaborator in the creation of mandatory government schools, Philip Melancthon, refers to "government as the common father," and schools as God's "chosen and rightful instrument in raising up such men." Those men, of course, being proper, obedient Lutherans. At its root, one can see that

these early schools were more about direction than
education. Rather than places where kids would be free
to learn and explore, they would instead learn to absorb
and repeat. Two common themes throughout Luther's
push for government mandated education were:
obedience to the government, and suppression of
dissent. The latter had always been imperative to Luther
as he was ruthlessly intolerant. After a peasant tax
revolt erupted in Germany in 1524 Luther proclaimed,
"let all who can, strike, slay, and stab them, in secret or
in public, remembering that nothing is more poisonous,
harmful, or devilish than a rebel." And as for the
government, "no breach of oath or duty could deprive
the Emperor of his right to the unconditional obedience
of his subjects." Nevermind the obvious irony, Luther
laid the foundation in Germany for a system of schools
designed to create a passive and obedient populace.
Gerald Strauss sums up Luther's ideal school system
perfectly in his paper, _The Social Function of Schools in
the Lutheran Reformation in Germany_:

> "Reformation schoolmen were anything but
> liberal educators, despite their devotion to
> the liberal arts. They were dismayed to see
> -as the preamble to one school ordinance
> put it- "the flower of our young men wasted
> by being allowed to live by their own will."
> "Not to let them have their will" (ihnen iren
> willen nicht lassen) was the essence of
> education, a process in which natural
> wishes, habits, inclinations, and tastes were

replaced by a higher volition, the will of
society's cultural masters."

The system of government run schools proved to
have staying power in Germany. Thirteen years after
Luther's death, the first mandatory state system was
established in Wurtemberg, Germany. Complete
nationalization of the movement was always periodically
interrupted by war, but then always retried, first at local
levels. Things remained this way until the 19th century,
when there finally became a truly national system of
mandatory, government-run schools in Germany.

We will return to Germany, as there lies the
direct ancestor to the American public school system,
but the later German system contains a dash of French
authoritarianism. In France, universal mandatory
education was established in 1791 as a principal part of
post-revolutionary life. It was a highly centralized,
national system subject to strict governmental controls.
One of the first edicts was that all instruction be in
French, rather than any of the various regional dialects
or languages that existed in France. This was a way to
reinforce nationalism and uniformity through schooling.
In addition, anyone who wished to work in the French
government had to provide proof that they had attended
one of the Republic's Schools. This made private
education that much less appealing. After the ascension
of Napoleon in 1804 the centralization of the school
system strengthened. In 1807, he declared:

"of all our institutions public education is the
most important. Everything depends on it,
the present and the future. Above all we
must secure unity: we must be able to cast
a whole generation in the same mould."

All schools would be put under government
control, with the newly established Imperial University at
the top of the education hierarchy. The Imperial
University had authority over primary, secondary, and
post secondary educational institutions. Similar to
modern day accreditation, a school could not be opened
up or operated unless licensed by the University. To
ensure uniformity throughout the system, all teaching
staff had to be licensed through government schools.
University officials would be appointed by the
government, and obedience to Napoleon's France
would be the primary objective of the system. The law
establishing the Imperial University stated:

"All schools of the Imperial University will
take as the basis of their instruction... fidelity
to the Emperor, to the imperial monarchy
which is entrusted with the happiness of the
people, and to the Napoleonic dynasty
which ensures the unity of France and all
the liberal ideas proclaimed in the
constitution..."

Similar to Germany, the French system was set
up to reinforce obedience to the government rather than

natural, organic education. Soon, a fateful military encounter between the two would ultimately influence the American school system for centuries to come.

It was late afternoon on October 14th, 1806 and Napoleon's army was in fast pursuit of a retreating Prussian force just outside Jena, Germany. At this exact time, a second German command arrived on scene intent on going on the offensive, apparently unaware of the retreat. The general of this second command, General Ernst Philipp von Rüchel, described as 'energetic but who lacked intellect', sent his forces charging directly through the columns of his fleeing countrymen. His troops ultimately ended up pursuing the same course of action as the first, retreat and heavy loss. It was a chaotic scene featuring a disjointed, sloppy Prussian army being routed at the hands of a more disciplined, well-managed French force. These were the Napoleonic Wars and this was the second major conflict in the series, known as the War of the Fourth Coalition. It took Napoleon less than three weeks to crush the Prussian Army and capture Berlin. The Prussian surrender was humiliating; substantial amounts of land and money would ultimately be ceded to Napoleon.

*A map of Europe during the Napoleonic Wars post 1812

This turned into a time of introspection among
the Prussian elite, and many saw it as a wake up call,
even a great opportunity. If Prussia (or any other
German state) was to free itself from French control it
had to reform; improve. It was feared by many on the
inside that Prussia was falling behind some of the other
powers in Europe, and from here we get The Prussian

Reform Movement of 1807. Unfortunately, many of the failures in Prussia were improperly diagnosed. Some of the Prussian elite looked at Napoleon's consolidated military control with admiration. As a result, further concentration of power was viewed as a remedy for the perceived inefficiencies of decentralized institutions. The reforms of 1807 covered everything from political unification to feudal arrangements to Jewish rights. Equally crucial among them would be systemic education reform, and here we begin to hear calls for a truly, purposeful national system of education. A system more in line with Napoleon's national hierarchical system would be favored over the previous patchwork of systems that defined the various German polities. An unvarying system of government-run schools would dominate the landscape in Prussia. Private schools would be permitted but under mostly the same regulations as the government schools as far as reporting, instruction, etc. The system was to be free, compulsory, and most importantly: uniform.

One of the most influential educational reformers in Germany at the time was a man named Johann Gottlieb Fitche. Fichte was a philosopher and professor at the University of Berlin, but became perhaps best known for laying out his vision for German education in his *Addresses to the German Nation*. Fichte's works are verbose and tedious, but not terribly difficult to decipher. Early on in his Addresses, he speaks pretty clearly as to whether his system would facilitate individual learning, or simply mold students:

"...someone might say, as indeed those who administer the present system of education almost without exception actually do say: "What more should one expect of any education than that it should point out what is right to the pupil and exhort him earnestly to it; whether he wishes to follow such exhortations is his own affair and, if he does not, his own fault; he has free will, which no education can take from him." Then, in order to define more clearly the new education which I propose, I should reply that that very recognition of, and reliance upon, free will in the pupil is the first mistake of the old system and the clear confession of its impotence and futility."

Fichte wrote and spoke extensively on education and there are a few common themes which run throughout his works; I'll crudely simplify them in to a few key points:

1. A uniform system of schools needs to be established nationwide with common instruction.

2. The schooling must be mandatory and available to everyone; opting out of the system should not be an option.

3. If designed purposely, a school curriculum has the ability to fashion and indoctrinate students in any way that it is wished.

4. The goal of the curriculum should be to create an obedient populace who willingly subordinate themselves to the state.

5. If the indoctrination is successful, the society can eventually run itself, in the government's vision.

The late John Taylor Gatto, perhaps the most influential voice in education reform over the past two decades, describes Fichte's vision here, from his book The Underground History of American Education:

> The ruler of Prussia called an emergency meeting at his palace of the wisest men he could assemble to discuss the problem and ask their advice; a philosophy professor at the University of Berlin, named Johann Fichte said the defeat had been caused by disobedient soldiers disobeying the commands of superior officers and following their own judgment; he said the time had come to bring into reality an ancient idea of treating the young like a school of fish, of habituating them from childhood to render total fealty to superiors by "school" training

that destroyed the ability to exercise free will, or even to imagine doing so, to transform young potential soldiers into machines incapable of disobedience by long compulsory school training and to correlate all future opportunity to how successfully each student accepted such schooling.

In his book The Impact of Science on Society, philosopher Bertrand Russell writes about nexus of mass psychology and education, where he apparently quotes Fichte from an 1810 speech, writing:

> The populace will not be allowed to know how its convictions were generated. When the technique has been perfected, every government that has been in charge of education for a generation will be able to control its subjects securely without the need of armies or policemen[2].

Fichte's sociopathic idea of schooling would soon be put into place throughout Prussia. It was a system designed not for children, but for adults. It was a system that would benefit the government by creating nationalistic, obedient citizens. It was a system that would benefit corporatists by creating compliant,

---

[2] While the line is in Russell's book, and Russell identifies Fichte as desirous of a system designed to indoctrinate, I've had trouble linking the quote directly to Fichte.

obsequious workers. It was a system that would benefit the military by creating tractable, steadfast soldiers. It was a system designed to ensure that none of these children grew up to question authority or think critically. And worst of all, it was a system that would be directly imported to the United States just a few decades later.

4. The Rise of Compulsory Schooling in the US

As was mentioned in chapter 2, the New England colonies are where we get the first taste of compulsory schooling in the United States. It would take 200 years, however, before any one state created a compulsory schooling law (Massachusetts 1852). It wasn't for lack of effort though; from the time of the Massachusetts Bay Colony, New England governments had attempted to force kids into schools.

The Puritan merchants who settled the Massachusetts Bay Colony in 1630 sought as much to reinforce Calvinist principles and suppress dissent as Luther did in Germany. This was important since the craftsmen, carpenters, doctors, and other laborers who were brought along for practical purposes were not all necessarily devout Puritans. John Calvin himself had previously set precedent for schools in Europe to be used as Calvinist indoctrination centers. In his indispensable book, <u>Education: Free and Compulsory</u>, Murray Rothbard writes:

> "...the major object for public schools was to inculcate obedience to a Calvinist-run government, and thereby to aid in the suppression of dissent. As a ruler of Geneva in the mid-sixteenth century, Calvin established a number of compulsory public schools in the city, and under his influence

Calvinist Holland established compulsory
public Schools in the early seventeenth
century."

Calvinist Puritans carried this attitude across the
Atlantic, and in 1642 passed the First Massachusetts
School Law which, in part, stated:

It is ordered, that the Select men of every
Town in the several Precincts and quarters,
where they dwell shall have a vigilant eye
over their brethren and neighbors, to see,
First that none of them shall suffer so much
Barbarism in any of their families, as not to
endeavor to teach, by themselves of others,
their Children and Apprentices, of much
learning, as may enable them perfectly to
read the English tongue, and knowledge of
the Capital Laws: upon penalty of twenty
shillings for each neglect therein.

Even in the militant, dictatorial atmosphere that
the Puritans had created at Massachusetts Bay, not
everyone was obeying the law. Five years later the
Colony redoubled their efforts and passed what became
known as the Old Deluder Act of 1647. Rather than just
mandate that parents ensure the literacy of their
children, the act forced communities to build schools
and send the kids there. The beginnings of distrust in
the individual and reliance on the State begin to become
evident. The Act stated that every town that grew to fifty

families be required to appoint a schoolmaster to teach literacy. Should a town grow to one hundred families, a grammar school was to be established and financed, primarily to prepare students for Harvard.

In the Puritan tradition, the schools were strict and unforgiving places. Children were expected to follow orders to a T, and if they did not, barbaric punishments often ensued (not surprising from the society which branded people with letters, burned "witches," and executed adulterers). One 18th century Massachusetts minister described being beaten constantly in school, for preferring play to work. Being particularly intelligent, he was put in charge of teaching some of the other children, and when they didn't learn properly he was beaten again. Schools being a place that make children miserable is no recent phenomena. It is precisely these beginnings which establish school as a place that is not meant to be fun, a place where play is only a reward for work, and a place where their natural faculties are to be suppressed in favor of the academic direction of much wiser overlords. Mandatory schooling continued in Massachusetts throughout the next century and was again authorized by the first state constitution of 1780.

Although it had the deepest roots, Massachusetts was by no means the only state to push for mandatory, government schooling. Early on in 19th century New York, five commissioners were selected to author a report on the creation of a system of state-wide common schools. In order to justify such a system they would have to establish that New York children were not getting educated on their own. Author EG West in his book, Education and the State, shows that the report indicated quite the opposite. Although school in New York was neither free, nor compulsory, still just about everyone was going. The report showed that literacy was widespread throughout the state with geography, not poverty, being the most severe impediment. Similar to the problems we saw in the early southern and mid-Atlantic colonies, sparsely inhabited areas had fewer schools than cities did. Here is where power hungry opportunists saw an opportunity to pounce. West identifies several reasonable courses of action which could have been undertaken, mainly furnishing aid directly to the affected areas. Instead, this isolated "gap" in school access was used to set up an entire system of schools across NY, regardless of geography, under direct control of the state itself. So, a problem confined to the rural areas was solved by subjecting the entire state to a system of government-controlled education. The first order of business was, of course, to create an expensive bureaucratic apparatus, complete with superintendents, commissioners, trustees, clerks, inspectors, and collectors. What's interesting, though, is that even under this Act schooling was still neither free nor compulsory in New York. People still had to pay rate fees to attend, and those fees were largely what made up teacher's salaries. Teachers hated rate fees, mainly because the administrative difficulty of collecting them fell to the teachers themselves. This could create a substantial delay in payment, or in some cases no payment at all. Their solution was not to seek more efficient methods of collections, but rather a Free School System across the state.

Teachers, of course, never indicated their own motives for establishing a government run system, they had to make it all about the kids. Many of the arguments they made in the early 19th century are almost identical to those made by union leaders today. There were three basic reasons given: the first was that education is a human right. This is fallacious for the same reason the health-care-is-a-human-right argument is today. Education is a positive right, in that it requires someone to act on your behalf, even if they don't want to. It outranks their liberty. Our country was founded on the basis of *negative* rights: we are free from others interfering with our life, liberty, or property. They do not require anyone to do anything for you, only to abstain from killing, enslaving, or stealing from you. Secondly, it was argued that the Free School System would reduce crime; in fact that is another common argument made today. This fallacy is self-evident; few could argue with a straight face that crime rates in impoverished areas have been improving over the last century and a half. Lastly, it was argued that a system of government schools would benefit the economy by lifting up poor people. This myth I need not get in to here as it is debunked in section II of this book. However, as I mentioned in Chapter 2, the material standard of living in America was already on the rise, and still rising before the imposition of government schooling. No, the real reason the system was desired was that tax collection by the state was more reliable than fee collection by teachers. It couldn't even be argued that demands from poor people were the impetus for state-run education. Through the first half of the 19th century, rate bills were the single largest source of revenue for most *rural* districts. The constant drone of "poverty being a roadblock to education" seems to fail here, and at a time when poor people were much, much poorer than they are today. People were still paying directly for education, even in the poorest areas of New York, before it was mandated to be free and compulsory.

Importing the Prussian System

Within years after the Prussian government implemented a system of state controlled education, Americans were travelling there and singing its praises. Edward Everett was the first American to receive a PhD from a Prussian University, he did so in 1817. Not coincidentally, Everett would later become governor of Massachusetts, which would later be the first in the Union to pass a statewide compulsory education law. Archibald Murphy, from North Carolina, told his state legislature about the wonders of Prussia, and wrote about how in public schools the "habits of subordination and obedience {should} be formed..." Scientist John Griscom went over in 1818 and also wrote glowingly about the Prussian system, specifically the pedagogic influence of social justice warrior Johann Pestaloozi, whom he met with personally. There were others, to be sure, but the remainder of this chapter will focus on two of the most influential proponents of the Prussian system: Calvin Stowe and Horace Mann, each with their own geographic sphere of influence.

Stowe pushed hard for the adoption of the Prussian system in the state of Ohio, and throughout the western United States at the time. He proudly proclaimed, "if it can be done in Prussia, it can be done in Ohio." In 1836 he had published, The Prussian System of Public Instruction: And Its Applicability to the United States where he wrote of "the wisdom and benevolence" of the Prussian system. Stowe spoke of the need to add education as a cabinet level position in the federal government; one of the first in the early republic to recommend this particular constitutional overreach. He goes on to outline a top-down system, virtually identical to the one in Prussia and the one attempted in France under Napoleon. In a passage with almost a Gestapo-feel to it, Stowe speaks of the need for appointed government officials who would regularly enter schools and report on their conditions to the proper authorities. He goes on further extolling the virtues of compulsory attendance in Prussia:

> "...all between the ages seven and fourteen are *obliged* to attend. No excuse, whatever, is admitted, short of physical inability, or absolute idiocy.... If the committee find that any child is negligent in his attendance, or does not attend at all, the parent or

guardian of such child is immediately
visited, causes of delinquency are inquired
into, and if the reasons are not satisfactory,
he is admonished to do his duty...and, if he
still continue negligent, he is punished by
fines, or civil disabilities; and, as a last
resort, where all other means have failed,
his children are taken from under his care,
and educated by the local authorities."

As would be the case with Horace Mann, Stowe
was particularly impressed with the program of teacher
training in Prussia. The Prussians took special care in
their hierarchical system to ensure the message was
uniform. Teachers would not, and could not, be
individuals. They would have to be selectively chosen
and trained by the state. Stowe explains how in Prussia,
each of the twenty-eight regencies was required to staff
at least one school for the education of teachers.
Candidates aged six to eighteen would be rigorously
examined as far as their aptness to teach, and in the
end issued a grade of either Excellent, Sufficient, or
Passable. They would then be placed by the
government, and could not decline a government
appointment. He likened the professional requirements
of teachers under the Prussian system to those of
soldiers, and admired the respect they commanded in
society. Stowe asked the people of Ohio to
enthusiastically accept a tax increase to make the
Prussian system a reality; he lectures them that the
amount they currently pay "is so small as to be scarcely

felt, and is nothing compared with the taxation of every other existing government." Indeed, Ohio would be one of the first western states to enact a statewide compulsory school law.

Seven years after Stowe's account of the Prussian system, Horace Mann took a trip to Europe to evaluate school systems himself. With Edward Everette (mentioned earlier) as Governor, Mann was appointed as the Secretary of the Massachusetts State Board of Education, the first post of its kind in the country. Mann was eager to see the system he had heard so much about for himself; in 1843 he visited schools throughout Great Britain, Germany, and northern Europe. As he would make clear in his Annual Reports to the Massachusetts State Board of Education, it was the Prussian system which he found most appealing. In the 7th report Mann writes:

> Among the nations of Europe, Prussia has long enjoyed the most distinguished reputation for the excellence of its schools. In reviews, in speeches, in tracts, and even in graver works devoted to the cause of education, its schools have been exhibited as models for the imitation of the rest of Christendom. For many years, scarce a suspicion was breathed that the general plan of education in that kingdom was not sound in theory and most beneficial in practice.

Referred to as the greatest of all American educationalists, Mann began to completely reform Massachusetts schooling as soon as he began his post as Secretary of Education. Just as had been done in New York, Mann erroneously referred to education as a *right* of every child, and that they could enjoy that right at the public's expense. In his Tenth Annual Report to the Massachusetts State Board of Education he went on to chastise those who valued actual property rights over made-up rights. Mann laments that the reason the US did not yet enjoy a system of free public education was due to "the false notion which men entertain respecting the nature of their right to property than in anything else." Mann questions whether anyone actually has "such an absolute ownership" over his possession that the government cannot come in and requisition them for whatever cause they feel necessary (yes, they do). Getting more hysterical, and seemingly desperate, Mann invokes the "Laws of God" to justify his free school system, and likens opposition to it as no different than infanticide. Much like modern day progressives, Mann had no patience for federal principals or the sovereignty of other states; Mann wanted his ideas imposed upon everyone else. When a neighboring governor, Chauncey Cleveland, entered office in Connecticut, one of his first orders of business was to repeal a public education law advanced by Mann's great friend, Henry Barnard. His reasoning was simple: people in Connecticut had always educated themselves prior to the law, and he saw no reason why they would not continue to do so in the future. The law, therefore, constituted nothing more than a waste of funds. Mann called Cleveland cowardly, spiteful, even *evil* for daring to govern his own state as he saw fit. Mann kept pressing in his own state, and in 1852 Massachusetts became the first state in the union which required all parents to send their kids to a public school:

> Section 1. Every person who shall have any child under his control between the ages of eight and fourteen years, shall send such child to some public school within the town or city in which he resides, during at least twelve weeks, if the public schools within such town or city shall be so long kept, in each and every year during which such child shall be under his control, six weeks of which shall be consecutive.

Just like Prussia, Massachusetts would create a tiered system of education, establish "Normal Schools" designed to train teachers, make the system compulsory, and fine parents for truancy. Neighboring states slowly began to follow suit, and by 1918 every state in the union had passed a law establishing a Prussian-style school system.

It is interesting to note that not everyone who visited Prussia was completely spellbound by their education system. Englishmen Robert Vaughn, founder and editor of the British Quarterly, wrote in a work titled the <u>Age of Great Cities</u>, that he looks "with much misgiving on the Prussian education system," and he goes on to explain precisely what many Americans were so perfectly willing to overlook:

> "...we venture to ask whether there be not some danger lest this new means of power over the popular mind, should become only another instrument of arbitrary rule, after the manner of the old, being used as a coadjutor of the old, in these disjointed times, or where that might not be practicable, be raised into its place? If national religions, in the hands of bad men, have been so often little better than so many mainsprings of state policy, may not national education be perverted in the same manner?"

As one observes the current, militant social justice curricula imposed upon our children, you cannot help but appreciate those words even more.

5. The Ugly, Nativist Truths Behind Mandatory Schooling in America

"Yet for all the abiding democratic idealism of the common school movement, it was motivated, well, by nativism." This is author and Harvard professor Jill Lepore, writing in her most recent book, These Truths: A History of the United States. American demographics changed more drastically in the first half of the 19th century than perhaps at any other time in the nation's history. This terrified many white, Anglo-Saxon Protestants, like Horace Mann, who had enjoyed social and political supremacy since the nation's founding. While Mann may not have been a devout Protestant, he was certainly weary of the non-Protestant influx of immigrants entering our eastern ports. There would be, unquestionably, a calculated, nativist undercurrent behind the push for public schools in the mid nineteenth century.

Between 1820 and 1850, the number of immigrants entering the country increased *fifty fold*. Continental Europeans were coming over en masse; the allure of cheap voyage, countless freedoms, low taxes, high wages, and available land sounded too good to pass up for many Europeans. In two decades between the 1830's and 1850's the number of Germans who came to America spiked from 10,000 to 200,000; they were apparently quite happy to leave their own despotic situation. Yet it was not the Germans that frightened

American Protestants, it was the Irish. Faced with a series of crop failures which began in the 1820's, the Irish left for America in extraordinary numbers. In the middle part of the nineteenth century no other group immigrated to America more so than they did. Protestants in this country had no tolerance for Irish Catholics. They were openly discriminated against, barred from employment, falsely accused of heinous crimes, and beaten up in public. For centuries, conspiracy theories about Catholic plots to take over America were even entertained. Such theories had legs beyond just a few oddball groups; extremely high-profile, respected Americans would propagate them. Samuel Morse lent credibility to the idea that Catholic European rulers were deliberately sending their citizens here to promote a political takeover. In fact, writes Lepore, to avoid such a takeover Morse believed the US government might need a secret cipher (although he eventually put the Morse code to public use instead). Lyman Beecher, father-in-law to the aforementioned Calvin Stowe, was among the first to suggest universal schooling as a way to shape the "uneducated mind" of the new foreign immigrants. In his 1836 publication, A Plea for the West, Beecher warns:

> "This danger from uneducated mind is
> augmenting daily by the rapid influx of
> foreign emigrants, the greater part
> unacquainted with our institutions,
> unaccustomed to self-government,
> inaccessible to education, and easily

accessible to prepossession, and inveterate credulity, and intrigue, and easily embodied and wielded by sinister design...What is to be done to educate the millions which in twenty years Europe will pour out upon us?"

On the other side of the country, one New York assemblyman cried: "We must decompose and cleanse the impurities which rush in to our midst. There is but one rectifying agent - one infallible filter - the SCHOOL." With Massachusetts leading the way, northeastern Protestants would urge the establishment of common schools as a socializing agent. What better way to Americanize, and Protestantize, this new populace than to force them in to Protestant schools?

While Horace Mann repeatedly spoke of the newly created public schools as non-denominational, economist Robert Murphy calls this "a farce," explaining how the schools used Protestant hymns, prayers, and read from the King James Bible. Mann's Massachusetts was becoming a Know-Nothing state, as was made evident in the 1854 state elections. The Know Nothings, later known as simply The American Party, had absorbed many people in Mann's defunct Whig Party. The Know Nothing platform was openly anti-Catholic, anti-immigrant, and anti-foreigner, and very much pro public education. As historian Tyler Anbinder explains his book Nativism and Slavery:

"...because Know Nothings believed that the surest method for guaranteeing the supremacy of Protestant values in America lay in promoting Protestantism in the public schools, educational matters occupied a significant portion of their legislative agenda."

These new nativist lawmakers immediately passed a law requiring *daily* reading from the King James Bible in public schools. The Know Nothing legislature also approved an amendment that ended public funds for Catholic schools; this economic warfare was designed to ensure an effective monopoly for the taxpayer financed, Protestant schools. And the financing for those schools was quite generous. The legislature would stop at nothing to fund their nativist goals; they not only increased the school tax, but the annual tax on cities and towns by *fifty percent*. To be fair, they at least split the cost with future generations by running substantial budget deficits. They attempted further, more draconian nativist laws, but only a failure to hold ⅔ the legislature stopped them.

As stated earlier, Mann was not a particularly devout Protestant, but he did end up with a religious-like embrace of the theories of phrenology; and it is very plausible that his enthusiasm for phrenology drove his push for public schools. While not religious, phrenology is equally nativist. Now a totally discredited medical theory, it enjoyed considerable popularity in Massachusetts in the 1830's. The idea was that certain faculties and acuities could be identified by the physical shape of the cranium. The northern European skull emphasized traits not endowed to the others. Mann was a passionate believer in phrenology and spoke energetically on its behalf. In turn, the Phrenological Journal of Science and Health spoke lavishly of Mann, especially his physical traits:

> Physically, Horace Mann possessed a delicate constitution. He was tall and thin, with light complexion and hair; his head was high and broad in front, especially in the higher intellectual organs, Causality and Comparison, showing a large predominance of the intellectual and spiritual faculties over the animal propensities.

Mann came to feel that he had a moral obligation to act on behalf of those not as physically gifted as himself; hence his fervent support for a free school system. Writing to a friend, he says:

> But on those, nobly endowed, to whom heaven had imparted he clearsightedness of intellect and the vehement urgency of moral power, he imposed the everlasting obligation of succouring and sustaining the first in their weakness and temptation and of so arranging the institutions of society as to withhold the excitements of passion and supply the incentives to virtue to the second class.

Mann, of course being the nobly endowed. And that institution of society? Of course, it would be the school.

6. The Growth of Schooling: the 20th Century

There were opportunities for the nation to be saved from the captive institution of forced schooling. In the early 20th century, John Dewey was extremely influential and said all the right things when it came to schooling: that it was dull, repressive, and the curricula was arbitrary. Moreover, it reinforced rather useless skills like memorization and repetition instead of inquiry or critical thinking. It turned out, unfortunately, that most of what he preached was a sham. Dewey was a socialist and saw the school as an opportunity, just as Fichte did a century before him. He was perfectly fine with a school system designed by radical progressives which reinforced progressive ideas. Indeed, for all his rhetoric, Dewey would do nothing to change the process of schooling, but much to transform schools into instruments of social justice.

As the nation grew and expanded, statists faced enforcement challenges with respect to forced schooling. As noted by the outstanding educational historian Michael Katz, mandatory schooling was basically unenforceable in its early stages. Western rural states had no realistic way of determining who was in violation of the laws, and rarely bothered to enforce them. During a seven year period in Montana not a single conviction was made under the law. This, too, could have been promising as politicians might have just scrapped the idea on the grounds of its impracticability.

However if you know anything about statists, you know they don't fold so easily. Thus begins what Katz refers to as the "Bureaucratic Phase" in mandatory schooling. States bulked up their enforcement mechanisms and the educational apparatus began to grow. This included the creation of extra rules, regulations, and officers to enforce them. The price tag was steep: between 1890 and 1930 total expenditures on elementary and secondary schooling increased by a multiple of ten. It would be around this time that states began tying their aid to school attendance; enforcement of truancy laws would become more and more militant. All of this new statute writing and enforcement, along with its dubious constitutionality, brought forth a host of legal challenges. We will conclude by looking at the role of the courts in the growth of government schooling.

The first major challenge to government schooling came about in Oregon, in 1925. By 1918 every state in the union had a compulsory schooling law, and was only a matter of time before one took the predictable step of banning private instruction. In November of 1922, the Oregon Compulsory Education Act was adopted, and would require parents (with a few exceptions) to send their kids to a *public* school. Failure to do so would be a misdemeanor. The Society of Sisters, a Catholic institution, along with Hill Military Academy, another private institution, was granted an injunction against enforcement of the law. The U.S. Supreme Court upheld the ruling, referring to the law as unreasonable. The opinion would properly state that:

"the child is not the mere creature of the State; those who nurture him and direct his destiny have the right, coupled with the high duty, to recognize and prepare him for additional obligations." This was an important early step in asserting the right of the parents and not the state to determine how their child is educated. The Court could have dealt a much more serious blow to public education but the same opinion affirmed the right of the state to regulate schools, examine teachers, determine what is taught, and ensure that kids attend *some* type of school. As the first major challenge to mandatory state education, Pierce ended up being a mixed bag.

Homeschoolers, it seems, have spent more time than others in court fighting for their right to educate. Many point to the homeschooling option as proof that compulsory schooling laws don't really exist, but do not realize how regulated homeschooling is. In Washington, parents who do not have enough college credits are not allowed to homeschool their children. In Massachusetts, no surprise, parents must get approval from their local school district to homeschool; moreover, students may be required to pass standardized assessments to prove equivalent education. This issue of equivalent education has produced some shocking judicial opinions protecting public schools. In 1937 a New Jersey judge convicted a couple for not providing equivalent instruction, on the basis that he could not:

"...conceive how a child can receive in the home instruction and experiences in group activity and in social outlook in any manner or form comparable to that provided in the public school....It does seem to me, too, quite unlikely that this type of instruction could produce a child with all the attributes that a person of education, refinement, and character should possess."

Thirteen years later, again in New Jersey, John O'Brien withdrew his two children, 11 and 8, from their public schools to homeschool them. The attendance officer in the county, Angelica Knox was let loose and the O'Brien's soon found themselves in court for failure to provide, again, equivalent instruction. In what seemed like an open and shut case, the Court was informed that Mrs. O'Brien had a Bachelors degree in Education from the College of St. Elizabeth, and had also had previously taught at three different schools in New York. Indeed, the Court found that:

The teaching material possessed by Mr. and Mrs. O'Brien, and such additional material as has been obtained by them from the public schools in Dennis Township, while not as complete as that used in the Dennis Township public schools, is ample in quantity and quality to meet the needs of fair teaching material in the third and fifth

grades respectively, and therefore, is
deemed to be reasonably adequate.

But again, statists are persistent. Even after the
O'Brien's had proved satisfactorily that they were
educating their children, according to the state's own
standards, they were still found guilty. In one of the most
stunning legal opinions you may ever read, it was held
that:

The entire lack of free association with other
children being denied to Mark and Eileen, by
design or otherwise, which is afforded them at
public school, leads me to the conclusion that
they are not receiving education equivalent to
that provided in the public schools in the third
and fifth grades.
The evidence convinces me, beyond a
reasonable doubt, of the defendant's guilt as
charged, and I do, therefore, find him to be a
disorderly person.

One relatively recent victory against state
overreach was sustained in Wisconsin v Yoder, 1972.
The state of Wisconsin came after an Amish community
who stopped sending their children to school after the
eighth grade. The state contended that they were
empowered, as *parens patriae* (meaning the
government is the legal protector of the children), to
extend high school to the students regardless of their

parents wishes. That claim was rejected on the grounds that it violated the First Amendment rights of the Amish to freely exercise their religion. In his opinion, as noted by Michael Katz in <u>A History of Compulsory Education Laws</u>, Chief Justice Burger makes some reasonably sound claims against all compulsory attendance laws, not just Wisconsin's. Arguably the best of those being that forced schooling:

> "..takes them {Amish children} away from their community, physically and emotionally, during the crucial and formative adolescent period of life."

The underlying foundation of that argument could easily be made on behalf of all children.

The next section of this book deals with schooling outcomes. To many, the outcomes are confusing. We sink so many resources in to our school system, how in the world can we rank anything other than #1? Understanding the history makes the results easy to understand. As I will point out, a system not designed for student achievement, unsurprisingly does not yield student achievement.

Part II: The Results of School

7. Define "Schooling"

Defenders of government run schools have offered a myriad of excuses as to why this system is not only needed, but is the best way to educate people. Interestingly, this has created a tenuous relationship between the state and the public school zealots. The latter cannot live without the former, but they also cannot stand the strings attached to the funding that props up public schools. Here in the state of Indiana, the Indiana State Teachers Association (ISTA) has led campaign after campaign against the Republican controlled House and Senate. The topics have ranged from low teacher pay, poor teacher morale and unfair teacher certification processes. Seeing a trend? Of course the pro public education defenders will espouse that it's "all about the kids", yet that seems to be a secondary matter to making sure their job is easy, well paid and they are set for life. This is just one of the many aspects of modern schooling that must be dissected. There are several other institutional disorders within public schooling that we will address in this section of the book.

As I explained in Part I of the book, the majority of American education has been propped up by government compulsion. There is a critical differentiation between education and schooling.

Education is generally understood to be the cultural transmission of knowledge from one generation to another. Prior to compulsory schooling, this was done in a very free and liberal way. Many cultures accomplished this by having children work in the home or village. They may have had the children work in what would now be labeled as apprenticeships. This worked well, up until industrialization. As urban centers grew and businesses started to sprout up, civic leaders felt the desire to mass educate children. While there was a small time frame of independent/local education, the move to government mandatory schooling evolved relatively quickly. In studying the historical evolution of education in America, we can identify the purpose of schooling, as men like Horace Mann, Calvin Stowe, Edward Cubberley, William Torrey Harris and others left their fingerprints on the social construct of schools. We also see the role of industrialists such as Carnegie and Rockefeller and their work in defining schools as preparation for the factory.

The experience and impact of compulsory government schooling on our children and families has been demoralizing. I will work to explain how the move to monopolized, compulsory schooling has been an unmitigated disaster. In order to do this, I will put the modern public school under a microscope. This calls for analysis of some of the most minute details that have a major impact on teachers, students and families.

So what does the modern school look like? There are many different aspects to address in order to paint the picture of how schools work and impact children. First we must address the physical buildings. Modern schools are draped in bland design, with little natural light, doors with no windows and now metal detectors and security protocols. Many social commentators have compared schools to prisons. This analogy is not simply powerful because of the forced nature of students being there. We will breakdown how the design of classrooms and buildings crushes the natural desire to learn.

Another factor in analyzing how schools operate is the children inside the building. According to the National Center for Educational Statistics, approximately 56.6 million children attended public schools in the fall of 2018. Each and every one of those students experience school in a different way. They bring various experiences, attitudes and desires to school. This, along with factoring the adults into the equation, creates an interesting dynamic inside schools across the country. I will examine the relationships between teacher and student. Increasingly, teachers have had a negative impact on children. Teachers have been complicit in labeling students as "special needs" or as having a medical malformity, usually in the nature of ADD or AD/HD. As we will find, these diagnoses are often just symptoms of children not playing the game of school the right way. In fact, according to a Michigan State University study an estimated one million children has potentially been misdiagnosed with AD/HD. That is almost 20% of all diagnosis.

Even more alarming has been the increase of negative physical activity between students and teachers. This can encompass physical and mental abuse, including that of a sexual nature. All of these factors are having a perverse impact on students and families.

Next, I will look at the methods and curriculum in schools. This is a very large subject to approach. It encompasses a variety of different subjects, ranging from how curriculum is determined to the way lessons are taught on a daily basis, known in the education world as pedagogy. In breaking this down I will address various aspects of the modern school, including; the testing culture, Common Core, and other curriculum programs and pedagogical methods for supposed effective teaching. All of these factors of course lead to a negative impact on the student. At the center of the curriculum and appropriate pedagogy is the main cog in the machine; testing. Students have been subjected to unbearable amounts of testing. These tests come in many different formats. Teachers will have you believe that the amount of testing students go through is all the government's fault. Afterall, many states have a formal standardized test that students take in an attempt to measure proficiency in areas such as math, language arts and science. While there are many issues with these tests, and the validity of them can certainly be challenged, teachers are also complicit in promoting the testing culture. Accepted methods today will have teachers administering multiple quizzes and tests on a weekly basis. While this is certainly not a new phenomenon, it is part of the larger debate over what constitutes good/effective teaching; a topic of great debate in educational circles.

Ground zero for the debate on best practices is the college classroom. Teaching colleges have been the beacon of pushing new and improved methods for teachers to use. Of course, these are simply recycled theories with shiny new vernacular. Couple this with school districts annual shifts in focus and it's no wonder teachers are so confused about how they should be doing their job. Each year teachers are led to a pedagogic approach which is different than the year before. All momentum is stopped, as new and improved models, curriculum and resources are pushed out by administrators. In the end, the student is the real loser. The constant changing provides no direction or focus on the process of teaching and learning.

Instead of allowing students the freedom to learn, what gets taught is how to conform to rules. Students are taught their place in the system and their place is to learn how to act. I owe it to you to illustrate what schools really teach. I will do this by looking at a prophetic piece written by the late, great John Taylor Gatto. Gatto eloquently lays out the real agenda of school in his 1992 masterpiece *Dumbing Us Down: The*

Hidden Curriculum of Compulsory Schooling. In analyzing this work, I will lay out the seven items Gatto says really get taught in schools and provide personal examples as support.

Finally, an examination of the results must be conducted. What has the return on investment been with public schooling? Various metrics can be used to demonstrate that this system has and continues to be an abject failure. Analysis at the surface level, shows how poor student performance and aptitude is on subjects taught in school. We will examine data from various tests administered to students. Beyond that, and probably more importantly, we will study the impact that schooling has had on our children. Each year more and more students are taking part in a system that not only does not accomplish its core goal of educating, but actively harms its participants.

Even students that appear to succeed in school actually leave with very few applicable skills and ability. The nonprofit organization GreatSchools led a study in 2018 that examined the causes and reasons why so many students are dropping out of college. According to the study, the number two reason, behind only cost, as to why students do not finish their undergraduate work is that they simply are not ready. The study goes on to highlight that nearly 60 percent of first year college students take remedial courses and less than 25 percent of those students actually graduate within eight years. This should lead every parent to examine what is going on in schools. Each year, all over the country, millions of students graduate high school with little to nothing to show for it. Those who are in the coveted "top 10" or even have the distinction of earning valedictorian may have really only shown that they mastered the art of "playing school." Again, all this should shake up every citizen and lead to calls for something else other than traditional public schooling.

As I present these ideas to people, the most common question I get is; what do you replace traditional school with? In the solutions section I will cover the ideas of what we can do to help stem the tide of damage that traditional schools have done. I will do this by looking at solutions in various levels, starting with analyzing the entire system, down to what an individual parent or teacher can do within a local school or home. Let's first start by analyzing attempts to simply build on what is already there through reform.

8. What About Reform

People from all interests and positions have been in agreement that something must be done to get better results from the schooling system. Teachers, unions, politicians and concerned citizens have all played a role in attempting to better public schools. This diverse mix of players and ideas has made coming to a consensus on solutions nearly impossible.

Since schools are operated by the government; politicians have had a major impact on school reform. Congressmen at the state and national level have attempted to introduce legislation, create initiatives and appropriate the correct amount of funds to improve schools. Presidents have continually tried to make education a priority as well. We can look back to the Lyndon Johnson presidency and the roots of "The Great Society". Johnson's attempt to fight drugs, poverty and remedy the inequity in education would set the stage for future presidents to engage in their attempt to "fix" education. The Reagan administration would produce the *Nation at Risk* report; George H.W. Bush would introduce the now infamous *No Child Left Behind* law and most recently President Obama introduced the *Race to the Top* initiative. Over 50 years and billions of dollars later and we are still trying to figure it out!

Ineffective public policy is not the only way politicians engage in education reform, we must also study the relationship between the politicians and the unions. There are various union groups that have made an indelible mark on the landscape of education. At a national level, unions like the United Teachers Federation and National Education Association have created precarious relationships with certain politicians (specifically democrats) that have often aligned school reform with the desires of protecting teachers. At the school district level, this often ends up pitting school administrators against classroom teachers and their union reps. At a national level, it generates debate that sees both sides taking shots to attempt to score political points. With both political groups and unions slugging it out over control, another group has emerged to attempt to reform schools; private donors.

While this is not a new phenomenon, we have seen an increase in the funding and influence of community leaders. These private donors are typically independently wealthy and socially active reformers. A majority of the big players earned their wealth in business or as hedge fund gurus. Historically, men like Carnegie and Rockefeller led the way to influence curriculum in schools. In modern times the Bill and Melinda Gates Foundation has been a torch bearer for these groups, donating millions of dollars to public and private schools that attempt to institute reforms. In fact, a Washington Post story in 2018 estimated the Gates Foundation poured in an estimated $215 million into a program that attempted to tie teacher performance to student test scores.

In a closer examination, it will become painfully clear that no amount of reform will save the school system as it exists. We must look to move on from thinking like reformers and start to examine options that completely reimagine the way in which we attempt to educate our youth. While education is considered "compulsive" or mandatory by the state, there are options for withdrawing from this broken practice. Some of these alternatives look very similar to the traditional model. Most people today are familiar with the idea of a charter school. These schools are often backed financially via a startup, much like what we mentioned above. Several states have also worked in public funding to support charter options as well. An example of a successful charter option is the increasingly popular KIPP Schools (Knowledge is Power Program). With the rise of the internet has also come the creation of online schools as well. Options such as K12, Inc. and Connections Academy have filled the demand for families looking for digital options. Other popular alternatives include self discovery or democratic methods of education. Examples of this are Montessori Models, the Sudbury Model and the Unschooling Model, which could include the homeschooling method. We will explain and analyze these options later in the book.

Obviously these alternatives to the traditional public school system come under intense scrutiny and attack by the pro public education crowd, including politicians, teachers and as an extension the unions. Anything that would threaten the livelihood of the education industrial complex (my take on Eisenhower's Military Industrial Complex) is going to be shouted down. This defiance knows no bounds. In recent years we have seen the spread of propaganda, marches on state capitals and outright intimidation to silence any opposition to public schools. Even the reformers within this group are guilty of these tactics. While their intentions are good, the results of their programs and plans would ultimately yield more of the same results. As Albert Einstein famously wrote, "*we cannot solve problems by using the same kind of thinking we used when we created them.*" So what is the best option to traditional schooling? I will spell that out at the end of the book. For now, I must start by critically analyzing how schools function today.

9. Testing... 1, 2, 3

The methods fed to teachers, first through teaching colleges and then through administrators is a cruel game. Year after year school districts cycle in new curriculum, typically built around some new focus on how to best get results from students. Each year I have been teaching, the school district I have worked for has had a "focus" for the year. These themes have ranged from implementing technology to understanding neuroscience related to how children learn and deal with stress. Of course with all this comes keynote speakers, new curriculum, professional development and other resources. All of these must be funded somehow. Yet we continue to hear year after year that there is not enough money in education. Despite the public battle for fully funding schools, what does not get discussed is the impact on teachers and students in constantly shuffling focal points. While these methods come and go and alter the way teachers teach and students learn, one thing has been a constant; testing.

Beyond well publicized state standards tests, there are national and international tests that give us a glimpse into how the United States stacks up to other countries. The well recognized PISA (Programme for International Student Assessment) test has continuously produced results that show how far behind American students are in areas such as problem solving, language usage and other critical thinking skills. What is important to note is that this not only shows a lack of knowledge, it demonstrates a lack of skill as well. These scores and results will be discussed later in the book.

While many standardized tests have been scrutinized for bias and being blamed for driving instruction, we do get some useful information from analyzing the results. Test scores highlight the systemic failure of schooling. Whether a state implemented Common Core (the highly controversial set of national standards implemented in 2010 as part of the Obama Administration's attempt to standardized what is taught and how) or created their own standards, the results yield one thing; failure. Even if you are a critic of using standardized tests as a measure of success, or lack thereof in schools, other metrics clearly show the failure of schools to educate. This includes increases in discipline records, dropouts/unenrollment and mental health diagnosis. Beyond the scrutiny that schools face for poor performance on these tests, this system is also having a major impact on the mental health of our children.

It should come as no surprise that schooling has a negative impact on the mental health of our children. Increasingly, children are being treated for various mental disorders including anxiety, anger, social distortion and suicidal tendencies. While educators are sounding the alarm bells about the lack of resiliency and coping skills students exhibit today, they are clearly missing the role school playing. According to the Anxiety and Depression Association of America, nearly 1-5 percent of students across the United States suffer from what is known as *school refusal*. This is defined as a disorder of a child who refuses to attend school or to attend school for a full day. This is often driven by school created issues of test anxiety, separation, teacher or peer trauma and forced transitions. The primary driving factor with this is test stress.

Beyond driving instruction in the classroom, standardized testing has also driven up anxiety among students. According to the Council of the Great City Schools, an urban school cooperative, students spend between 20 to 25 hours per year taking standardized tests. This obviously does not account for how much time students spend preparing for these tests. In addition to preparation, students must perform classroom tests or what are known as summative assessments. For example, last year my son in third grade took between 3 to 4 tests on a typical Friday, including reading, spelling/vocabulary and timed math facts. Having all these tests piled on one day not only creates a tremendous amount of anxiety that day, it builds throughout the week.

Beyond the stress and anxiety created by testing, students are also struggling to fit in socially as well. One of the defensive points that pro public education people make is that school promotes social skills. However, studies are showing the negative impact that school has on a growing number of children. In particular, schools are struggling with problems of bullying, harassment and exclusion. This is not limited to peer to peer interaction. According to a 2017 study conducted by The Children's Center for Psychiatry, Psychology & Related Services an estimated 4.5 million students grade 8 through 11 are victims of some sort of sexual misconduct from an adult. It is no wonder when we look at just these two factors alone, that an estimated 23% of students have been prescribed medicine for mental health issues! With all this in mind, we must consider what a school day look like for students

It's What's Inside That Counts

There is no "typical" student experience, contrary to what some may say. Every student has unique experiences. The first and most obvious place to examine what schooling looks like is to describe not only the layout of the system, but more closely to discuss the buildings. One common term used to describe public schools is with a "one size fits all" label. This can be applied to the concept that many kids, obviously of different abilities and interests, are pushed into a singular classroom at one time and "taught" lessons on various subjects. We will analyze teaching methods later, for now we will analyze the physical buildings and discuss the impact these structures have on our children. This is important, because it plays a major role in understanding just why forced schooling is so harmful to our children. Often times we hear of crumbling infrastructure, unsafe buildings, lack of funding, etc. We are not denying that this exists, but it certainly can vary from building to building, district to district, city to city.

As you travel across the country you are bound to notice the urban and rural landscapes peppered with schools. Depending on what part of the country you are in, you may notice some structural differences. However, a school is a school, right? Yes, it is true some may be constructed with different materials. Some may be newer than others. Some are one story low sprawling buildings, some are more compact, two story builds. There are also differences between inner city and rural schools based on physical space and other geographic constraints. Most people in education will try to sell you on the belief that rural and suburban schools are far superior to urban schools in terms of the physical condition of the building and education resources available.

This line of thinking may be summed up best in a 2013 *American Psychological Association* article by Dr. Cynthia Hudley. Dr. Hudley lays out the case that many students (families) in urban environments are struggling economically and this economic disadvantage not only creates an unfair circumstance, but that the system is inherently rigged and keeping them in poverty. In her own words "The American mythology continues to insist that education is the path to the middle class for those struggling to escape the grip of poverty." (Hundley,

2013) She goes on to paint the picture of urban schools that lack resources such as appropriately credentialed teachers, outdated computers and technology, crumbling physical structures, etc. Finally she wraps up by discussing the stress that this puts students under and draws a connection to how this negatively impacts learning. Indeed, many hardline pro public school educators will present this scenario when attempting to explain why urban schools perform so poorly.

This line of thinking is so pervasive in the world of education, that it is not even questioned. However, it is simply a myth. Several studies have been conducted proving that urban students are more successful than their rural counterparts. According to a study done by the Programme for International Student Assessment (PISA) from the same year as Dr. Hudley's article, urban students in OCED (Organization for Economic Cooperation and Development) countries outperform those who grow up in rural environments. The study contributes this to many factors, including; more resources, better economic opportunities and greater autonomy for how schools distribute resources. This can lead to the result of an advantage of half of a school year.

In addition to physical differences of the buildings, there are differences in ability, background and personality that all factor into how students experience a day in school. This does not even take into consideration interactions with peers and other adults, which of course is different for every student. Increasingly these experiences are having a negative impact on children. A simple Google search will tell the story of teachers and school personnel that are charged with neglect, sexual misconduct and dereliction of duty. The data and stories should have every parent disgusted.

We must also talk about the mental anguish that students experience through bullying. While schools across the nation have attempted to tackle the problem in the wake of school shootings, there has been very little impact. Even though we may not be able to build out a standardized experience or typical day, we can examine some common interactions and events in the course of the day. What impact do these have on our children and how do they effect the learning process?

So schools are schools. Some may look different, but when we peer inside the walls, we see there really is not much difference. What is the result of this? Whether or not inner city schools perform better or worse than rural schools is really just a diversion from the larger issue that schools in general are set up for failure. Instead of spending valuable time and money resources on trying to build out the perfect building, we should be discussing the damage that forcing children into *any* building, regardless of the condition, does to a child. I have had the privilege of observing many different classrooms during my ten plus years in education. After going in and out of schools I could almost tell you down to the smallest details what a classroom setup would look like and the bottom line is no matter what accoutrements are used, students are not learning!

The Classroom

So what does a school room look like today? I can tell you as a former student in the mid 1990's to today as a teacher; not much has changed. I like to use an analogy that famed businessman Marcus Lemonis used in a special episode of his show, *The Profit in Cuba*. Upon arriving to the island, Lemonis is painting a picture for the audience of what life is like in Cuba. Part of this is explaining the physical structures; the businesses, homes, cars, etc. In performing this task he paints a grim picture by surmising that Cuba looked like it was stuck in the 1950's when the Americans generally fled from the Castro Revolution. Now imagine the same principle being applied to what the American classroom looks like. It probably is not much different from when you attended school, no matter your generation. Public education proponents will lecture community members, teachers and students on how different students are today than they were 10, 15 or 20 years ago, yet the general classroom structure remains in tact.

To highlight just how inadequate classrooms are today, let's examine a typical high school language arts/humanities classroom. Without fail, we will see the traditional classroom desk. Arrangements may vary in terms of standard 6x5 box sets versus pods of four desks lumped together or possibly partner tables. Some teachers have embraced using alternative forms of seating, such as "Starbucks" tables, wobble stools and even couches. In any event, the student will be seated in a manner that has their attention toward the front of the room, focused on a whiteboard/chalkboard or possibly some type of interactive display screen such as a SMARTBoard or Promethean board. More importantly for the teacher is the focus on themself. The physical dimensions of the room will more than likely impact the overall layout, but this is typical. The room may or may not have windows to allow natural light. Many teachers have moved away from using the overhead lighting to using a softer lighting from vertical lamps. This is supposedly meant to bring a calming effect to the room.

In addition to the physical layout, you are almost certain to observe the walls plastered with rules, school mottos, behavioral/disciplinary reminders and schedule(s) peppered in with a variety of motivational quotes and inspirational statements. Finally, you will find a bevy of bookcases with hard copy material that is either out of date or no longer being used. This also brings up the fact that in many of these schools there is a textbook room that is likely to be filled with volumes of textbooks, novels and other print material that sit collecting dust.

Obviously classrooms are only one part of a

school building. We cannot forget the sterile hallways, peppered with lockers and the ubiquitous inspirational quote bulletin boards. We must also examine lunchrooms and common areas. It will not take much imagination to determine what these will look like. There are some schools that utilize an "open campus" for lunch. This is where students are generally able to leave to a common area during lunch, but they are still supervised while eating, and if we are going to lay out the design of the physical lunchroom, we must also analyze the food. Bland would be an understatement. Staying in line with the idea that children are not well enough equipped to make decisions on their education, the state also determines that students cannot make their own decisions on what they eat. With the introduction of the Choose MyPlate program in 2011, First Lady Michelle Obama drastically overhauled "choices" that students have when eating a meal at school, banning sodas, salt and outlawing high fat foods brought in from home. Again, the main takeaway here is the control over the choices, or lack thereof, that students have related to school.

Why spend the time discussing the physical layout of the modern school? As you paint this mental picture in your mind, think of the impact this has on the student. Students are crammed into desks from 45 to upwards of 75 minutes at a time, four to seven times a day. The experience is mind-numbing. Simply being cooped up in a building all day is bad enough, but the sterile environment makes it all the more troubling. It is no wonder that students are diagnosed with ADD or AD/HD. It is also no wonder why students have such a low opinion of their school. They are subjected to taking courses they have no interest in nor, as research shows, will they benefit from. To add the cherry on top, the methods that teachers use are outdated and do little or next to nothing to stimulate learning among students. Teaching is a function; not a profession. Bellringers, Do Nows, Pair-Shares, Webquests,PowerPoint lectures, Worksheets, Project Based Learning, on and on it goes. No one ever stops to ask the students what they want to learn or how. Why would we? Afterall, isn't this the function of "experts".

10. Deciding What to Teach

Whatever is learned in classrooms across this country, one thing is certain; students do not retain it. Dr. Bryan Caplan clearly spells this out in his book *The Case Against Education: Why the Education System Is a Waste of Time and Money.* In discussing the problem of fadeout, Dr. Caplan explains "human beings poorly retain knowledge they rarely use." (Caplan, 39) Further, he cites a study conducted in 2016 that found most people that take high school algebra and geometry forget about half of what they learn within five years. He goes on to highlight how severe the problem is in literacy and numeracy as well, citing a 2003 study by the Department of Education of 18,000 adults that produced alarming numbers. Only 13% of respondents demonstrated proficiency in Prose, Document and Quantitative tasks. This trend continues when we study History/Civics. For example, only 24% of 1,000 Americans that completed a *Newsweek* survey knew that the U.S. Constitution establishes a republican form of government. It is clear that students do not retain this information because they do not care about it. Why should they? What does a high school student gain from being forced to take Algebra, learning a foreign language or enduring a fine arts class?

Notice the emphasis on *force.* We are not advocating that students not take these classes, but clearly every student is going to have different interests and strengths. Why not allow students the opportunity to take classes that are interesting to them, or on their own timeline. What if Timmy isn't ready for Geometry until his senior year? What if Jane is an amazing musician and wants to develop skills related to performing arts? We will cover this in greater detail in the solutions chapter. No matter how we answer those questions though, the point is, the results documented above are putrid. Why? The pro public education crowd will default to the normal talking points; not enough money, teaching to the test, politicians setting curriculum that they know nothing about, etc. If this is true, let us examine the curriculum and instruction presented in schools today.

One of the great mysteries of public schooling is determining *what* gets taught to students. Over the history of compulsory schooling, the curriculum taught in school has traditionally been based on a mix of local authority, relationship with the business community and governments at both the state and local level. These ever changing, moving parts have made it difficult at times to determine what is best for students to learn and know upon completing school.

Early foundational teaching in America rested on the idea of teaching "the three R"s", commonly referred to as reading, writing and arithmetic. One room schoolhouse teaching would drive memorization of facts into children's heads and accounts of the experience quickly show us this way of learning is demoralizing. A 2009 EdWeek piece by Kathleen Manzo highlights what life was like at Highland Springs Elementary at the turn of the 20th Century. She provides excerpts from a journal written by former students that categorize the old one room schoolhouse as "...like a prison." She goes on to quote historian Herbert Kilebard, author of the book *The Struggle for the American Curriculum: 1893-1958*. In his book, Kilebard describes the environment inside the school stating that students would rather experience "factory labor to the monotony, humiliation, and even sheer cruelty that they experienced in school." (Kliebard, 1987) It does not take very long to get a picture of what it would have been like to be in this type of learning environment. On top of the methods used, the lack of teacher knowledge and training made things even worse.

The American landscape changed drastically from the early 1900's through the 1930's. This was a period of American history where we saw a rapid rise in urbanization. As society was changing from agrarian to industrial, people began to settle in cities and around the factory. Schools were not only growing in size, but were being looked at to provide students with the skills needed to supply adequate labor. There were two main drivers of this movement; government and big business. Men like John Dewey, John Rockefeller and Andrew Carnegie would leave an indelible print on the landscape of education curriculum. Noted educator and activist John Taylor Gatto points out the cruel reality of what men like these had in mind as they influenced the education world. In his book *Weapons of Mass Instruction,* Gatto calls attention to a mission statement from the Rockefeller General Education Board that reads:

> "In our dreams...people yield themselves with perfect docility to our molding hands. The present educational conventions [intellectual and character education] fade from our minds, and unhampered by tradition we work our own good will upon a grateful and responsive folk. We shall not try to make these people or any of their children into philosophers or men of learning or men of science. We have not to raise up from among them authors, educators, poets or men of letters. We shall not search for embryo great artists, painters, musicians nor lawyers, doctors, preachers, politicians, statesmen, of whom we have ample supply. The task we set before ourselves is very simple...we will organize children...and teach them to do in a perfect way the things their fathers and mothers were doing in an imperfect way."

What a chilling, yet bold, statement that so clearly resonates with what public school has become today. We see this demonstrated in

statements about students viewed as "lost
causes" These students are tracked and labeled
as cooperative candidates; students who do not
have the academic fortitude to be in the
classroom a full day, so they work half a day.
Sounds noble, until you realize the true intention
is to rid the teacher of a headache. As much as
we want to place the blame on various levels of
government, we see here the tentacles of the
businessman shaping education all the way back
in the early 1900's.

The history, design and intent of building a
nationalized schooling system has been laid out.
However, we must address the specific impact of
curriculum reform, as it speaks right to the heart of the
failure of the system. The attempt to reform curriculum
over the decades is a microcosm of the larger systemic
failure of public schooling. In the same EdWeek article
mentioned above, Manzo chronicles the attempt to
modernize education curriculum during the 1930's and
40's. Curriculum was being dissected and redesigned
to meet the ever changing needs of students and
society, but much to no avail.   It is fascinating to see
that the issues that were being dealt with in 1945 are
still being wrestled with today! Manzo writes "A study
commissioned in 1945 by the U.S. Office of Education…
concluded that many schools were failing to design
programs for the 60 percent of students who did not
participate in either college-prep or vocational
programs." (Manzo, 2009) Not only were education

experts not able to hit the mark with meeting the needs of students, many saw attempts to modernize curriculum as "foolishness". In the end, students and society as a whole have suffered. Students have been led to believe that they must take "x" number of classes or earn "x" number of credits by taking classes that will have little to no impact on their lives.

In addition to early reform attempts, standardized curriculum has ruled the day of the modern classroom. Indeed, many defenders of public education will lament that they are handcuffed by standards such as the most recent redesign known as Common Core. Moreover, teachers must contend with administering standardized tests. Teachers will often complain of having to "teach to the test". They are right! Most math, language arts and science classes are now all geared around teaching to either a state mandated test or end of course assessment test. There are multiple ironies in this though. Standard practices encourage teachers to assess students in an almost nonstop manner. Between formative and summative assessments, students will be continuously providing feedback on what they have supposedly learned throughout a lesson or unit. This begins to snowball as students not only complete checks for understanding, traditional homework, projects and quizzes/tests. Once again we must acknowledge that it is the system, not necessarily the people that is inherently flawed. Regardless, it must be addressed and those that defend it must be held to answer for why they believe this system is the best one for educating our youth. Least you think it is just the curriculum that is flawed, let us examine the pedagogy of teaching.

Teaching How to Teach

Failure in schools is not from want of trying. You have to give it to the pedagogic experts, who routinely cycle through the new flavor of the year in terms of what will turn around and save the system. In my decade in public education I have been exposed to numerous attempts to reconfigure the way I am supposed to teach. When I first entered the classroom in 2007 I was inundated with information on Bloom's Taxonomy. Of course it was presented as groundbreaking and the one thing that would engage students and generate more excitement in the classroom. As I would later find out, the original concept was introduced in 1956 by educational psychologist Benjamin Bloom. This pedagogic construct has been altered several times, including the introduction in 1997 of Webb's Depth of Knowledge. Webb's framework was designed to get educators to consider how to get students to think about content more deeply. Inevitably, new handouts were made, laminated cards distributed and we were told this would be the emphasis when our evaluator entered the classroom for observations.

A year or so passed before yet another shift came. This time the focus was on using technology in the classroom as many school districts were rolling out iPads and Chromebooks and the new directive was to focus on using the SAMR model. SAMR stands for substitution, augmentation, modification and redefinition. SAMR is supposed to encourage the educator to contemplate the role of using technology in a lesson. Again, I was a participant in numerous training and professional development sessions on how to implement this new pedagogic practice.

Now fast forward to today. This last school year we were introduced to the concept of educational neuroscience (EN). The concepts behind EN are focused around understanding the way the brain works. Again, not a new phenomenon, yet cloaked in the idea that students today are under more stress than they ever have been. Acknowledging this and analyzing what triggers a student's emotions is supposed to help them calm down and focus in school. Additionally, we have been told to integrate focused attention practices and brain breaks into our lessons. I was personally told this year that no one activity should run over 20 minutes without a brain break. We were also encouraged to start or refocus a class with a focused attention practice, such as; closing your eyes and imaging colors or listening to waves crash while practicing rhythmic breathing.

What is the big deal you ask? These seem like solid practices. Look at it from this perspective; what does it say about school, curriculum and teaching strategies when you must perform these tasks, simply so students can function in a normal state? In several staff meetings we were encouraged to think about the stress, trauma and emotional baggage that students bring to school. We were told it is incumbent on us to build connections with these students and help regulate their emotional states all in the name of earning a grade. What educational leaders fail to ever address is the stress and anxiety caused by school itself! This is the problem with all these educational practices, they never square up the real problem; compulsory schooling. The moment force is introduced and freedom is removed, all bets are off. This is not a cop out or excuse for kids to be lazy. It is a maxim that holds over the history of human existence. People learn best when they are free.

Ever since this curriculum reform movement out of the early 20th Century, the government has not only increased their control over nationalizing curriculum, but they have continually been reactive to world events to try and rationalize reform. From Lyndon Johnson's "Great Society" to end poverty, to Ronald Reagan's "A Nation at Risk" to keep up with the Russians, all the way down to George Bush's "No Child Left Behind" to attempt to close the achievement gap, we continually see the national government reacting to what the data shows as a failed attempt to educate our children.

We can debate the layout of the typical classroom and what it should or should not look like. We can have discussions over curriculum and what types of classes students should take. However, there is no need to study charts and graphs to observe just how much of a failure our schools have become. All we must do is study our children. We can see how bored they are taking meaningless classes. We can see how anxious they are with continual testing. We can see how destructive it has become to label children as ADD and AD/HD and placing them on medications to turn them into zombies. All of this, along with lagging data and what college professors and business leaders are telling us about how unprepared students are upon leaving high school, tells us that American schools have failed.

11. What Should Be Taught

At this point it should be nearly self-evident that American schools are failing our children. If you have any doubt this is true, study this data that John Taylor Gatto presents in the previously mentioned book *Weapons of Mass Instruction.* Gatto discusses the damaging effect that schools are having on youth by analyzing literacy rates through the military from World War II up to Vietnam. According to the United States Army, of the 18 million soldiers that were tested, 96% demonstrated proficiency in reading. By the time of the Korean War, those numbers fell to 81%. Fast forward to the Vietnam War and over 25% of those checked were deemed illiterate, incapable of reading safety instructions, interpreting road signs or deciphering orders (Gatto, p. 9-10). Each one of these groups of men should have presumably received better instruction than the next, yet the results clearly indicate a problem.

You might think this was simply a blip on the radar or a problem unique only to the military; unfortunately this is not the case. Gatto goes on to highlight issues with other metrics used to measure competency and accomplishment through schooling. SAT scores were commonly renormed and more disheartening are the impacts on minority students that go through the public school system.[3] These trends

---

[3] For more on this, search *The Achievement Gap*

continue today, as we hear about how unprepared students are for college or the workforce.

In his 2008 book *The Global Achievement Gap*, author Tony Wagner lays out the case that our schools are missing the boat on teaching students the skills they will need to be successful in the 21st Century. Wagner weaves in stories of interviews with various business leaders while also recounting research he conducted in visiting school districts across the country. The results were not surprising to anyone who has spent time analyzing how schools operate. As Wagner visited several school districts and classrooms he documents the disengagement, boredom and apathy that runs rampant in schools today.

One example he provides comes from a series of classroom observations he performs within a district superintendent in a New England region school. He sets out to look at the best of the best. This district is a well off one, with the median family income around $175,000 (Wagner, 55). Wagner also mentions that this particular school is one of the best in the state with some of the highest standardized test scores in the nation. His observations took place in several honors and Advanced Placement (AP) courses. The results were not shocking to me, as an educator. A summary of the six classroom observations paints a picture of boredom, lack of interest and very basic memorization and recall skills. The overall synopsis is that there is no clarity to lessons being taught. Teachers and students are simply going through the motions. Tasks are being completed and checkboxes are being marked, but there is little to no cohesion to the lesson. Who can blame the actors? Both parties know how to play the game just enough to get by.

More alarming is the lack of applicable skills that are missing. Earlier in his book, Wagner lays out what he calls the Seven Survival Skills for Teens Today. These are:

- Critical Thinking and Problem-Solving
- Collaboration across Networks and Leading by Influence
- Agility and Adaptability
- Initiative and Entrepreneurialism
- Effective Oral and Written Communication
- Accessing and Analyzing Information
- Curiosity and Imagination.

Reflect back on what we learned earlier about the way the classroom operates and how lessons are taught. None of these skills are being achieved with the methods used in modern schools. This is an enormous problem for students as they enter into college or the workforce. It is high time we shift from stuffing our students head with useless knowledge, and equip them with skills they can use to start and advance a career.

I have had the opportunity to visit many different classrooms during my teaching career. In 2015 I spent a year as a Technology Integration Specialist for a company that partners with school districts to streamline technology processes. A significant part of that business model grew when schools began to implement 1:1 classrooms. I started by rolling out Google Chromebooks to a rural district in grades 5-8 and eventually incorporating grades 9-12. From there I would go on to work with 4 other school districts in the state. As we partnered with the districts, we would perform an analysis known as an instructional audit. We would pop in to classrooms across the district in all building levels. We would start by analyzing various levels being observed on the SAMR Model. SAMR is an acronym I mentioned earlier in the book that analyzes how technology is being implemented in the classroom. We would watch teachers and students for about 15 minutes each and try to observe teaching methods in general, but more specifically focused on technology integration.

First, I believe it is important to acknowledge that these skills cannot be "taught". They can be acquired by allowing students the chance to apply and enhance them, but they cannot be taught in a traditional lesson. I can say with a high degree of certainty that very few if any of the Seven Survival Skills were being addressed at any given time in a lesson. The model of teaching in schools today simply does not allow for it. There is no room in preparing for the standardized test, whether it be the End of Course Assessment, standardized state test (here in Indiana that test is known as iLearn) or the end of year AP test. Instead what we continue to see in 2019 is the same methods that have been used for over the last 200 years.

Classroom lessons by and large are still teacher focused with chalkboards now replaced by an interactive whiteboard, complete with digital screen to access information from the internet, including video. Some teachers see it as progressive that they have moved from lecturing to simply letting another expert do the heavy lifting. Students are numb to this. I can attest to this firsthand, as on occasions that I tell my students we are going to watch a video it is met with eyerolls and apathy. Again, earlier in the book I addressed what the typical day looks like for a student. Imagine experiencing this hourly, daily, weekly, monthly, etc. It is no wonder why students report that classes are boring and unengaging. It is also no surprise why attendance rates are so poor as well. While students may miss extended periods of school for a variety of reasons, such as; chronic illness, family trips and religious ceremonies, stress and anxiety are a major factor. According to the Department of Education it was estimated that over seven million students missed 15 or more days of school—the number the department uses to designate "chronic absenteeism." I can personally attest to students who have missed 15 or more days in a single trimester (13 weeks)!

12. What Is Actually Taught

John Taylor Gatto was good at what he did. He was an educator in the state of New York for 26 years where he was named New York City Teacher of the Year on three separate occasions, culminating in being awarded New York State Teacher of the Year. In 1991, Gatto abruptly left his teaching career after issuing a shocking op ed piece to the Wall Street Journal. In his piece titled *I quit, I think* Gatto explains that while he has amassed all the accolades of being a "great" teacher, what he has really been doing is harming children. How could Gatto, who had won the highest honor in education in his state, claim that he was actually hurting children?

When we reflect on what happens at school, whether as a former student or possibly as a parent, we may recall things like taking tests and completing homework or making friends and playing sports. While there very well may have been some good in going through school, the foundational experience of school leaves much to be desired. Even more than that it can be downright sinister. After he left teaching, Gatto went on to expose people to the dangers of public education. In 1992 Gatto wrote a tour de force piece entitled *Dumbing Us Down: The Hidden Curriculum of Compulsory Schooling*. In this work Gatto lays out what really gets taught in school. He lays out seven foundational things that schooling teaches children:

- Confusion
- Class Position
- Indifference
- Emotional Dependency
- Intellectual Dependency
- Provisional Self-Esteem
- One Can't Hide

Reading through Gatto's list will leave you shaking your head; not in disbelief, but in agreement. We'll return to this list a little later, for now we will examine the response from parents and community at large.

Unfortunately, we have fallen asleep at the wheel when it comes to assessing the work being done in our schools. If we look to critique schools at all it may be to analyze standardized test scores. Here in the state of Indiana, the Department of Education maintains a database of student performance in the aggregate. Each school is also awarded an A-F letter grade, which effects the image and even funding of the school. If parents look deeper, they may analyze funding metrics, academic offerings and resources such as technology. Of course many parents will spend time critiquing the quality of the teacher their child gets in a particular class or grade level. This is probably giving parents too much credit. In fact, as I prepared for this book I took time to ask ten parents in my community what they thought about the schools. Eight of the ten parents stated that they never or very rarely thought about the "quality" of the schools. This was followed up with six of the ten admitting that they had little or no contact with school personnel throughout the year, beyond basic communication with the teacher. Additionally, there were two sets of parents that told me they had to contact the teacher on multiple occasions with one even going to the principal. When asked what precipitated the communication, they stated it was due to a bullying situation. Finally, I asked parents what their overall impression of the schools were. Nine of the ten stated they were very satisfied with the schools. Only one said they were dissatisfied with the school.

Indeed these beliefs hold up in scholarly work on parent attitudes toward school. In a research study conducted by University of Northern Illinois professor Lee Shumow entitled *Parents' Educational Beliefs: Implications for Parent Participation in School Reforms* 61% of parents surveyed believed the primary role of school is the transmission of skills from teacher to student. Moreover, parents attitudes toward teachers shows that parents have turned the keys to the car over to the teacher. Shumow explains that parents see their primary role in education as a support or encouragement to what the teacher is doing. It may not be surprising then that so few really care about what truly is going on in school, or to reflexively think about the impact that school has on children.

Putting all this together can help a parent feel good about the experience their child will have in school. The problem though is the shortsightedness of it all. As we have maintained throughout, the fundamental problem with schooling is the foundation of it. All of the items listed above and the various accoutrements are simply that; they are window dressing. What Gatto does is to strike at the heart of what schooling really does to not only the student, but to the parent and teacher as well. Let's break down the seven things Gatto lays out with a personal update since the list was revealed back in 1992.

Confusion. Gatto starts by identifying that the curriculum that is taught in schools is driven by randomness, which leads to confusion. This confusion is fueled by over teaching. Essentially Gatto believes we teach students too many random ideas and useless facts. This makes connecting the dots very difficult for children who are trying to make sense out of what they are learning and why they are learning it at a given point. This is absolutely accurate. Take for example the state standards of a typical middle school course. I have pulled a statement illustrating the randomness of what is taught in 8th Grade Math:

> *"The Mathematics standards for grade 8 are made up of 5 strands: Number Sense; Computation; Algebra and Functions; Geometry*

*and Measurement; and Data
Analysis, Statistics, and Probability.
The skills listed in each strand
indicate what students in grade 8
should know and be able to do in
Mathematics."*

Do you see the randomness? Ask the questions; Why
do students need to learn about Algebra and Geometry?
What does it mean to "know and be able to do
Mathematics? What is the connectivity that students are
supposed to experience in taking this class? Instead of
connecting concepts to life experiences, students are
left frustrated and confused by the randomness of all
these ideas being thrown at them. In addition the
disconnected nature of curriculum continues as students
move from class to class. What connections are
students to make from diagramming sentences in one
moment to solving word problems in math the next?

Class Position. Next, Gatto states that one of the
principles transmitted to students is that they are mere
numbers. This is accomplished in a variety of ways.
The most dangerous manner in which this is
accomplished is through ranking students by test
scores, homework scores and grade point averages.
This creates groups of students; the "smart kids", the
"dumb kids", the "special needs kids" and so on. This
teaches kids their place in school. It teaches them envy
and spite. Of course another effort of labeling kids with
a number is through assigning them a grade level. This

teaches kids that they are expected to have obtained a set of arbitrary skills by various ages and grade levels or else something is wrong with them. This is done under threat of force through holding the child back or taking away some other intrinsic reward such as socialization opportunities. Moreover, and perhaps even more damaging, is the segregation of students based on class position. At any given time you can walk into a classroom and see students broken up into groups based, not only on ability, but on academic labeling. For example, I have from time to time volunteered in my two boys elementary school. On multiple occasions I would observe students pulled out in small groups. These students were identified as "strugglers", those who needed additional support or help. Sounds noble, right? At an early age, students probably do not cognitively recognize this. However, as they get older they most certainly come to understand who the kids are that struggle based on grades, test scores and other numeric labeling that get applied to their classmates.

Indifference. This is perhaps the most damaging part of what gets taught in school, as it kills the process and love of learning. What did Gatto mean by teaching "indifference". He describes this as molding students to conform to the bell system used in schools. What a damaging tool, the bell system! In constructing lesson plans, teachers are led to believe that they must create lessons to span "bell to bell". What a farce! When we condition students to stop whatever learning may actually be occurring at a given time, simply because a bell has rung, we kill their desire to learn. We are communicating to them that what they are really doing is not all that important. The signal over a bell tells them that something else is more important or pressing; something they may have zero desire to participate with. Ultimately this creates an attitude of indifference in students, creating a zombie-like attitude of simply "going through the motions".

I can personally attest to seeing this firsthand. Being a high school teacher and specifically of seniors, I see many students who are disillusioned with school. This is much deeper than the typical attitude of "just ready to be done". This is a feeling that they are wasting away; wasting time, talent and abilities. Many of the students who illicit these feelings are the ones we would identify as high ability or gifted and talented. I recall a conversation with a student, I'll call him Josh. Josh was one of those students that would show up for class and on his best day, he would go through the motions. On his worst day, he would sleep or watch YouTube videos. Trust me when I say, this was not due to the fact that he could not comprehend the content. In fact, there were many times that he would come to me before or after class excited about an article he had read on a website or prepared to discuss the latest video he watched on economic principles. There was desire and passion there… and then the bell rang. That bell did more to kill Josh's love of learning than any other systemic rule or regulation could ever do. This was a kid that I would routinely find trying to convince his classmates why they should read more about Libertarianism during passing periods and lunch. He even gave a copy of Smedley Butler's *War is a Racket* to one of our teachers to read. However, get him to comply with completing work and it was a totally different person. This is the power of teaching indifference.

Emotional Dependency. While indifference kills the learning process, emotional dependency breaks the will of the child. Gatto lays out the myriad of ways in which the teacher holds the power, "by stars, and red checks, smiles and frowns, prizes, honors, and disgrace, I teach kids to surrender their will to the predestined chain of command." (Gatto, 6) I wish this was as simple today as it was back in 1992. Today this idea of emotional dependency is far darker and more sinister. It has reached a level where teachers are going beyond the level of providing positive feedback or criticism. Earlier I cited a study by the American Psychology Association that stated over 4 million students have suffered some sort of sexual or physical abuse at school. As is the case with most abusive relationships, one party normally fills trapped. In this case it is obviously the student, who feels helpless to report this behavior. Again, this pushes the narrative that an emotional dependency has been created, just as in the classic battered wife syndrome. Additionally, schools are now employing educational neuroscience. We implemented this curriculum in the district I teach in last year. Exactly what is educational neuroscience? Essentially, EN is an emerging field of scientific study that uses cognitive and developmental psychology, educational psychology and other forms of education study to attempt to understand how people learn and deal with trauma. Our main focus this past year was understanding the brain and how it works. We spent time teaching our students the anatomy of the brain and breaking down what each part of the brain does in regulating emotions and breaking down information. From a staff perspective we were encouraged to build relationships (beyond just the typical classroom interaction) with our students. One example of this is an activity called a 2 x 10. In this exercise, the teacher is to have a 2 minute conversation for 10 straight days with a student. We were encouraged to hold conversations on topics that would be of interest to the student. This may sound well intentioned, but again it highlights the concept of teaching emotional dependency. It sends the message that no one at home cares about you, or you are a problem in school, so I am going to try to fix you. What is the source of this? The teacher of course, which the student becomes dependent on to seek acceptance.

Intellectual Dependency. It would only make sense that if students become dependent on teachers for emotional approval, they must also look to teachers as the source of knowledge; the only way they can learn. Gatto informs us of the long lasting impact of this. He posits that what this does is models that students must always default to an elder in finding an answer. It squashes the desire to seek answers independently and instead forges dependency on adults to tell them what to think. Gatto goes on to state that those who learn to play school successfully are the ones who learn not to question things. Push back will not be tolerated. More recently this has taken on a new form where technology has in many ways changed the methods for communicating lessons from teachers to students. Many districts in my state, including the one I currently work for, are 1:1 districts, meaning each student has a device (a Chromebook in my situation). While this sounds like a great opportunity for students to access information in an efficient manner, what it usually leads to is teachers using technology to simply find information. Earlier in the book I referenced the SAMR model, which is a construct to assess the ways in which teachers use technology. In my time as a classroom teacher and technology integration specialist, I can confidently say that most teachers use technology at the Substitution level, or the first level of integration. Very few are able to move beyond that and use technology to challenge students to create or redefine the targeted learning objective, again creating a dependency on the device to provide an acceptable answer.

Provisional Self-Esteem. This ties back to the emotional dependency that Gatto previously addressed. However, the key difference is that the provisional self-esteem is achieved, once the student his/her will broken and conforms to what the teacher wants. Gatto also discusses the idea of parent involvement with this as well, as teachers send reports home on a regular basis that either illicit approval or dissatisfaction based on what the teacher states the behavior of the student is like at school. Again, I can personally attest to the validity of this, as I am constantly nudged and encouraged to reach out to the parents at the moment I believe the student is not conforming to the rules of school. At this point the student will now have two sets of adults "teaming' up on them. This sends the message that confidence is questioning methods or pushing back against the way things are down in school will not be accepted. Buried in all this is that all forms of reflection come from someone other than the student. Self reflection plays no role, because it would give power to the student, which we cannot have!

One Can't Hide. In this final item that Gatto addresses he aptly summarizes the true intent of what school is really all about; surveillance. From the moment a child enters on a school bus to come to school to the time the deboard for day, they are under constant watch. Teachers are trained to not let kids out of class, except in cases of emergency. The hallways are chocked full of cameras. Moreover, teachers are encouraged to intermingle with students during the limited social time (passing periods and lunch). Students are never out of reach of the teacher or administrators in the building. The ultimate message with this; no one can be trusted. It's no wonder students create "burner" social media accounts. These are secondary social media accounts that allow students to express their true feelings and beliefs. The final piece of the equation comes in the form of homework. Gatto calls this the extension of the overwatch produced by school. It ties that bond between teacher and parent to assure compliance by students. Questioning the motives of the work or pushing back means that there is a fault in the child and that cannot be tolerated.

13. The Results Are In

So this is the modern school system. Contrary to what you will hear from public school advocates, this is the real account of what schooling is all about. More and more people are waking up to the shortcomings of this system. To this point, we have intentionally tried to illustrate the negatives beyond just test scores, which are routinely used as the measuring stick for public school achievement. The primary reason we have avoided referring to test scores is due to the inherent bias in the tests. Most states use some form of standardized test to assure all students are learning the same material, at the same time. The writing and administering of these tests are chocked full of flaws, ranging from how questions are formulated in test creating to the manner in which tests are administered at the schools.

Perhaps the most asinine part of standardized testing is the arbitrary pass/fail scores. Take for example ISTEP, the Indiana Statewide Test for Educational Progress. The Department of Education sets minimum and maximum scores, along with what are identified as "Pass" and "Pass+" scores. The state has set English/Language Arts scores for grade 3 as 428 (Pass) and 500 (Pass+). Beyond asking the question of what these results tell us, the more pressing issue is what the scores communicate. At 427, the student is a failure, but at 428 they are proficient. One could argue that there has to be a definitive cut line, but the greater point is; measuring aptitude in courses through standardized tests probably isn't a good thing for teachers or students. While there are holes in these metrics, they are an unfortunate reality of school today and they do shed light on how fundamentally flawed the schooling process has become.

In state after state the stories are the same; students are falling behind and not meeting standards set forth by the state. Take New York for example, according to Cornell University's NYC SchoolData program less than half of all 8th graders in the state are proficient in English Language Arts and Math. We see this same type of result across the country. Indeed these results do not stack up well internationally either. A 2015 Organisation for Economic Co-Opertation Development report shows just how far behind American students are falling. The average score for 15 year olds in Math, Language and Science on the Programme for International Student Assessment (PISA) test for the U.S. was a 470. Only Mexico (402), Chile (423) and Turkey (420) had lower scores. Thirty-one other nations had scores higher than the U.S., with Japan leading the way at 532.

Again, public school advocates will cry foul for using this type of data to make judgement statements on them. As has been mentioned on numerous occasions; we are not blaming the people, we are attacking the system. What seems odd is the lengths that teachers and other advocates of public schooling go through to trash the system, only to turn around and prescribe more of the same!

Is All Hope Lost?

Let's take a deep breath! Is all this overwhelming to you? Does it open your eyes to what *really* goes on in schools on a daily basis? I highly doubt you have ever thought of school in these terms. Sure, as a parent you may have had frustration with a teacher from time to time or struggled in helping your child with a homework assignment. Maybe you have even been in the principal's office having a spirited conversation about your child. Have you thought about it from the perspective provided above? Or, as most parents likely do, have you always thought your child was the issue? It's time to start pushing back and questioning the methods of these schools. I have attempted to provide you with the data and first hand experience to demonstrate the danger of forced schooling. Not only are schools killing students' love of learning and amounting to a severe crippling of human capital, in the worst of cases it is physically, mentally and emotionally harming our children. I'm sure there are positive things occurring in schools. As much as I have seen the negative, I have also seen positive. I have seen students take ownership of their learning. I have seen students capitalize on cooperative programs that provide them with invaluable experience as they transition into the next phase of their life. However, the evidence is overwhelming that this system is damaging and while there may be many parents that want to continue to partake in this, alternatives must be analyzed.

While the government has a monopoly on schooling, there are alternatives and there are options we believe to be superior to public schools. In this final section of the book we will take you through the solutions that we find far superior to the neighborhood school.

What Are Our Options?

Throughout this book I have made it a point to differentiate between schooling and education. I have also made an attempt to define, in various ways, the impact schooling is having on our youth. It would be very easy to sit back and continue to list criticisms of the system and offer no solutions. That is not my desire. While I am critical of compulsory schooling, I also know that if we want to see any real, substantive change we must engage in promoting alternative solutions to the current model. I also want to be very clear in stating I am not advocating to force families away from public schools. Instead, what I am calling for is a removal of compulsory schooling laws. A return of power back to the family would be the most desirable result. In fact, I have written about this in the past; addressing the issue of educational control through the subsidiarity model. This is a framework that calls for political decisions to be made at the most local level possible. In other words, if an issue can be solved at the town council level, there is no need to go to the state level seeking resolution. In our opinion, applying this to education would result in returning all decision making related to education children back to the parents.

In many states there are degrees of power parents have in choosing educational pathways. While many options require parents to follow state guidelines, there is a growing tide of educational liberty. We are going to present you with three alternatives to your local public school district; homeschooling, charter schools and self-directed learning centers. All three of these are available to families in some manner. In this section we will provide a brief history and overview of the option, along with examples of how the alternative is superior to public schooling.

The third and final section of this book is dedicated to solutions we have to offer relating to the current public school model. This section is intended to be a collection of thoughts on alternatives, choices and actions that parents could make regarding the education of their child(ren). We want to be blunt; these solutions are not perfect. No human system is going to be flawless. We do contend that these alternatives are far superior to public schools. There is no secret to why these are better. Unlike the government run school system, none of these solutions are founded in force. The American schooling system is fundamentally flawed for this reason. When the foundation of an organization is defective, the entire system will fail. Because of this, reform is a futile exercise. Progressives have attempted to reform this system for over 150 years. We have diligently attempted to lay out the results of this reform. When we discuss these results with people, we typically hear objections:

- *If you abolish schools, won't people stop learning?*
- *If you don't force kids to go to school, what will they do all day?*
- *So you're just going to let people go uneducated*
- *How will kids learn socialization skills?*

The list goes on and on. Why is there so much push back against breaking down the pubic school monopoly? Is it fear of change or a lack of imagination? Probably more sinister than either of these is the stranglehold of power and money. Schooling is a racket. Pause and reflect on the variety of businesses that have their tentacles attached to the public school system. Walk down the aisle of your local Wal-Mart and count the number of companies represented in the traditional "back to school" supply list. In addition to these companies, organizations such as; Pearson, McGraw-Hill, Cengage, Houghton/Mifflin/Harcourt, Google, Apple and many others stand to profit from the government schooling pyramid scheme. Other industries have seen big spikes in sales by being engaged in the business of education. Insurance for digital devices, digital device accessories, education consultants, engineers and construction companies. The lists go on and on. In all the K-12 school system cost taxpayers $694 *billion* in fiscal year 2017 according to the United States Census Bureau. This was the largest increase in public school funding since 2008. Can you start to see why there might be such hesitancy to break up the monopoly?

Nevertheless, there is a movement at the grassroots level to push back. In several states charter schools are gaining ground. Homeschool numbers are consistently growing as well. More recently there has been a movement toward self directed options. We will provide you with insights on these options and why they are superior to the local school. The following is a collection of essays we have written with potential solutions to "one size fits all" approach of public schooling.

What is Education without School?
A Guide to Self-Directed Education

As we have established, there is clearly a difference between schooling and education; with schooling characterized informally as a system that molds children by teaching them conformity and in the process crushing their love and curiosity of learning. This is a very unnatural process, and while schools have failed in many areas, disengaging students from learning has been a smashing success. The methods schools use are relentless. It starts early (and now unfortunately even earlier with a push toward universal Pre-K) by teaching conformity to rules instead of allowing personal development. Public school apologists will defend this by stating that children need to learn to follow rules and obey. As they grow, students are subjected to social stratification. In school, this is accomplished by labeling students as; special needs, bottom 20%, needs improvement, gifted and talented, honors, and so on. This teaches children they have limited abilities and everything else that proceeds from here is based on these labels. Another ill effect of labeling is placed on children that are identified as having a disorder, such as; ADD, ADHD or the infamous "OHI[4]" label which can include a myriad of issues. Diagnosing children with these "illnesses" is a huge deal

---

[4] OHI is the acronym for Other Health Impairment

for schools, as students who receive these labels are worth three to four times as much in funding. All the while, the psyche of the child is trampled. The worst position to be in at school is to not qualify for the special needs label, where at least you may get a chance at receiving additional support but also not play the game of school well enough to be seen as having extraordinary skills to qualify for honors courses. That's right, being in the middle of the road, or the silent majority is where educational dreams go to die. The invisible student that school absolutely fails. Never in trouble, but never motivated by the endless parade of worksheets, arbitrary projects and mind numbing busy work, these students waste away their one and only opportunity to pursue their interests. In short, schools are geared to teach to the extremes.

Education in contrast to this, is viewed as the opportunity to learn in almost any and every situation. Life, itself, is an education. This is the principle of open source learning. Imagine, if you will, a child that wakes up every day and has creative control over what they learn, when they learn it and how they learn it. Does this sound unreasonable? Of course it does, because you, like many others have been conditioned to believe we cannot possibly rely on children to tell us what their passions and desires are in life. We have bought in, hook, line and sinker to the notion that they must be molded, as I explained above. Have you ever challenged that notion? That is what I hope to accomplish with this essay. Challenge the misconception that children are too stupid, dumb, unmotivated and irresponsible to take control over their own learning. As I spell out what this might look like, you must break down the barriers that have been built up to keep you from visualizing how this will not only work, but allow our children thrive; allow them to regain their love of learning and allow them to experience what truly being educated feels like.

It has been stated that you cannot give anyone an education, they must take it. What this statement communicates is simply everything that is wrong with compulsory schooling. We force children into classrooms for 180 days a year. By the time they will have graduated a child will have spent over 2,000 days confined to a school building, shuffling in and out of desks, completing tasks that amount to virtually nothing. What would the child look like, how much would their life be altered, if we took those 2,000 days and simply let life run its course? Wouldn't children stop learning? Wouldn't they sit around and Snapchat, play Xbox and eat Cheetos all day? This is the default thinking that I challenge you to change. You cannot conceptualize children learning independently, because you have been led to believe school is the only way that can happen. I propose that it can and should happen. This process would be very natural and achievable through breaking down the monopoly government schools have established.

How do we begin? First, we must break down

compulsory schooling laws. We must return decisions on how to best educate children to the family. Reclaiming power the national government has seized in controlling education is a must. All decisions should return to the states, and more importantly to local communities. Doing this would effectively allow parents choice in determining what is best for their family in pursuing education options. While it is possible to currently reject the local public school, doing so requires jumping through many hoops and is not feasible for many families. In addition, the established power of unions, backed by politicians, has done a wonderful job of preventing options from threatening the monopoly. This power struggle is on full display in states like Arizona, where family groups for school choice have become more vocal, only to meet stiff resistance from state and national unions.

In addition to breaking down compulsory schooling, we must also work to define what is learned through the educational experience. Obviously, in an environment where there is no force, the child and family will be defining what is learned, when it is learned and how it is learned. This is anathema to public schooling, where bureaucrats and so called experts have determined the scope and sequence of learning. This does nothing but create strife and anxiety as children are pressured into hitting "benchmarks" or producing standardized test results. The outcomes of these are what are used to produce the dreaded labels that are branded onto the child like a giant billboard for all their days in school. This starts at an early age, by forcing children into buildings and getting them "ready to learn". This is a farce. In fact, there is mounting evidence that early learning does not produce better learners, and in fact it may indeed be counterproductive. Dr. Peter Gray, professor of psychology at Boston College notes that several studies support this claim. Dr. Gray writes in part;

> "Early academic training somewhat increases children's immediate scores on the specific tests that the training is aimed at (no surprise), but these initial gains wash out within 1 to 3 years and, at least in some studies, are eventually reversed. Perhaps more tragic than the lack of long-term academic advantage of early academic instruction is evidence that such instruction can produce long-term harm, especially in the realms of social and emotional development."

This is just the tip of the iceberg when it comes to determining the methods of teaching in school. Students in schools are forced into classrooms at arbitrary times and taught a disjointed set of "standards" that leave them frustrated and confused. What is the purpose of telling a high school Freshman that they must take Biology? Why does a Senior *need* to have taken an Economics and Government class to graduate? Think of the human capital that is wasted.

This is the time where the student could be exploring career pathways, working in internships and networking with career contacts. Instead they are bored, anxious and upset being prodded into classes that amount to no positive experience for them or the educator. If we strip this away, how can we be assured that learning will occur?

We must take on the responsibility for helping guide our child's learning. We can complain all we want about the shortcomings of public school, but let's face it, we have turned the keys to the car over to the government in terms of educating our children. In fact, many naysayers of this option will claim that if children are not forced into schools the parents would not have the capacity or ability to provide their child with the proper environment to learn. Moreover, those same critics will point out that this model will not meet the needs for families in terms of educational choice. Here is a popular criticism; If children are not forced to attend school, many disadvantaged families will be left with no options. What about the inner city, poverty stricken family? How will they be able to afford private school options? Again, this is typical of framing the issue around the current environment and not seeing a different perspective. It fails to acknowledge the myriad of choices that would arise once the government monopoly is torn down. It is very likely that several organizations would arise to meet this specific need. Moreover, we are not calling for the complete abolition of public schools, only that our government stop forcing families into this option.

So what might some of the choices look like once compulsion is removed. As it stands now, some options include homeschooling, charter schools, private schools and self-directed learning centers. Of these options, I claim the self-directed model offers the best environment for children to blossom in their learning. Let us now explore the structure of self-directed learning.

First and foremost, self-directed education rightfully returns power and decision making back over to the family. Beyond that, it provides an environment where students and families, in tandem, can make decisions about an overall education pathway. Note that I included *student and family* in the description. One of the most popular objections I hear to self directed education options is that children will not know what they want or will not be motivated to learn. First, I contended that this is only true insofar as the current model has zapped this power from them. Once removed, I believe we will be shocked by how motivated and passionate children can be and are about learning.

Second, removing the cloak of structured curriculum is not as dangerous as it may seem. Often times standards and assessments are simply a waste of time and are fruitless. Giving students autonomy on how they learn, how they demonstrate what they have learned and when they accomplish this will produce a much better result for all parties involved. This is the secret of the sauce that is self-directed education. Break the constraints that schooling creates from the mind of the child and they will be allowed to flourish. The earlier we can implement this, the better. As Kerry McDonald points out in her book *Unschooled: Raising Curious, Well Educated Children Outside the Conventional Classroom* there will be an adjustment period once a child is removed from the schooling culture and introduced to a self-directed model. During this period of time it is vital that the child be given space. As the child gradually begins to experience freedom, it is incumbent on the adults and peers in their life to help guide them in the discovery of what they want to learn. Again, the key here is being free of coercion.

How can this possibly work? There are numerous examples of how successful self-directed education can be. One current model that is in place is the Sudbury School. These are schools that are democratically run, with a very light staff that serve simply to help guide and aide students in their education. Students take total control in forming the day to day operations model. A key component to the learning methods used at Sudbury schools is learning through experience. This could include unstructured play time, apprenticeships and networking or taking formal courses taught by contracted educators. Activities can vary day to day in a self-directed school. It is difficult to describe what a typical day might look like. This can vary from center to center and even within a particular learning center each day may be filled with a variety of activities. A reflection of several centers shows the diversity and freedom available to students. Most centers require students to arrive within a time period early in the day. There is usually a student led meeting to discuss internal affairs. After that, students are free to engage in activities of their choosing. This may include; creating art, playing music, playing video games, engaging in debate or simply creating stuff through using equipment like 3D printers. In this structure, natural curiosity and experience are the guiding factors, not random curriculum or teacher led lessons.

Another great benefit of this model is the democratic nature of the system. Those engaged in self-directed learning are encouraged and bound to build connectivity with one another. This develops a web of potential learning points that allows every person involved from the student to the learning center director to promote a positive learning environment. Imagine the amount of growth and pride this creates. Indeed there are numerous testimonials to the benefit of this system. There are currently about 10 Sudbury schools scattered across the United States. In addition, there are other similar democratic, self-directed learning centers that employ a model very similar to that of the Sudbury model.

Again, this is just one model. There are many other options to push back against forced schooling, but self-directed options are gaining momentum. A quick search of the Alliance for Self-Directed Education website reveals the overall growing popularity of this option. As I mentioned in the outset, no system is perfect and I would certainly not advocate forcing people in this direction. I would however encourage anyone who has reservations about the current one size fits all approach of government schooling to explore the self-directed model.

Answering the Critics

The most common question I get when the subject of eliminating forced schooling comes up is, "what would you replace it with?" My favorite response is to paraphrase the great Thomas Sowell: *when the doctor takes cancer out of your body he doesn't ask what you want to replace it with*. But before I get into the specifics of the "replacement," let me take a second to explain two reasons why this is an unfair question to begin with.

Learning is an innate, organic faculty. We are all born curious; we explore the world around us from the time we are born in an attempt to learn and understand our surroundings. Learning does not begin at a specific time or end when a bell sounds. It does not require worksheets, lectures, books, standardized tests, or arbitrary letters and percentages. It simply requires the inherent spirit of curiosity already gifted to each of us. Before any of us were placed in institutional forced schooling we learned far more than at any other part of our lives. The Centre for Educational Neuroscience tells us that most learning happens between 0 and 3 years old. This has been the case for every human ever born, anywhere, across all time. It is forced schooling that is new. Forced schooling is an unnatural, government-created institution which attempts to dictate the terms of learning. It fails miserably and it always has; kids hate school. That one fact has been constant across time and culture. They love summer, they love weekends, but hate returning to school. They do not hate learning though. Never has a kid explored something borne out of his own curiosity, formed a new understanding, and rejected the process as dull or boring. They may brush aside the new understanding as unnecessary or useless, but that is done on their own terms. Social oligarchs supplanted natural learning with schooling, so why is the burden placed on us to explain how we would replace schooling? Instead, the supporters of forced schooling should have to defend their institution. They should have to explain why a coercive institution is better for cognitive development than natural exploration. They should have to explain why memorization is a more useful skill than following natural inquiry. They can't; the institution is indefensible if learning is the metric. Given what I laid out in part II of this book, there is no question why they deflect the onus to our side. In fact, many times when attempting to defend forced schooling its champions end up defending the *employees*, and not the kids at all! We hear about all the jobs that would be lost, the economic impact, and so on. So the appropriate question is not what would I replace schooling with, but rather, why did you replace learning with schooling?

Secondly, asking me to describe the "replacement" is asking me to predict the future; sorry, I can't. This would be like going back to the 15th century and complaining about the inefficiency of travel under the ox/cart system. If someone shot back: "well if you don't like the ox and cart, what would you replace it with," no one could be reasonably expected to predict the combustible engine, air travel, etc. I don't need to have an on-demand prediction of future society under a deregulated, decentralized system of education. That is not my question to answer; the market will satisfactorily answer that question if we are just patient enough. What I do know is that human ingenuity will bring about innovation and advancement just as it always has. The same structures that brought food, transportation, and technology to the masses will also educate them.

So while I prefer not to answer the question at all (since I cannot actually answer it), I realize that most people would find that unsatisfactory. To continue, I'll do my best to describe what I think a world without forced schooling would look like.

A few summers ago my sons expressed that they were interested in learning how to swim. Some friends of ours would invite us over to their pool, and while their kids would dive carelessly into the deep end, mine were confined to the shallow end dependent on flotation devices. As they watched the other boys swim freely, my kids developed a natural desire to learn swimming. My wife and I went on the internet to read reviews of local swimming programs. We also asked friends who had sent their kids to swimming lessons. We settled on a fitness club in town after evaluating cost and reputation. I was put in contact with a swimming coach and she asked me for my objective. I told her: I want the boys to be able to get to the side of the pool should they accidentally end up in water that is too deep for them to stand. She said she could do that in 6 lessons. We agreed on the price and the times, and the lessons were scheduled. After 6 lessons I was reasonably satisfied with the results. I felt confident that my kids would be able to save themselves in an emergency situation and we opted not to continue the lessons. In the future, if my kids have the desire to become more proficient at swimming we will return for more lessons. In short, this is one way in which I think education would look different if it were completely deregulated. Skills would be offered on an a la carte basis and families would choose how much or how little of the skill they wanted to learn. Traditional schools would likely still exist, for any family that wanted more of a rounded, liberal arts education. The only difference is that they would be non mandatory. I am often accused of wanting to destroy public schools, I don't. I want to destroy the law. It is the market that will determine whether traditional schools continue or not. But many people, kids especially, do not see the value in what they are forced to learn at public schools. Therefore, they never learn it at all. Many kids memorize things so that they can score well on a test, but they do not learn things they don't care about. When kids want to develop a skill, they work hard to develop it. They practice it to become proficient and continue learning until they feel they have learned enough. There is no reason why they could not learn math or language arts the same way.

What about poor families? By creating a system of direct payment, are we not just creating a system of education solely for the rich? Even worse, a system to reinforce racial disparities? Let me deal with the second question first, since it is more hysterical and easier to answer. First off, just google *racial achievement gap education* and look at any one of the options that appear; they will all basically show the same results. That's what the government schools have achieved. For all the talk, the money, and the effort that go directly into "justice" and "equality", the government schools have created a racially stratified system evident by its own results. A decentralized system would not deal with *groups*, it would deal with *individuals*. Government schools obsess over groups; they lump all kids who look the same into a statistical group regardless of the varying interests and abilities within that group. In the government schools you are either a Black student, Hispanic student, Asian student, White student, or mixed race student. Their policies cannot possibly work because they do not target the kid, they target groups, as if each group is just a homogenous band of interchangeable parts. Market arrangements are about voluntary interactions between *individuals* who both value the arrangement. Certainly the freedom for prejudicial behavior exists, but the incentives do not. The need to cooperate voluntarily with one another makes racism costly and unnecessary. I do not need to go through it here, because it has been well documented by Milton Friedman, Thomas Sowell,

Walter Williams, and countless other great economists, but free access to both product and factor markets has reduced racial disparities in economic outcomes. A system of deregulated education would yield the same results; at the very least it could not be any *more* racist than the outcomes of our current government schools.

As for the poverty issue, I would have to concede that most families, not just poor families, would not be able to afford schooling in its current form. But that is the problem: its current form. Schooling is a government institution with access to the public coffers. Many public schools are extravagantly wasteful establishments, driving up the cost to educate attendees. High schools have Olympic size swimming pools, sports fields of all kinds, state of the art media centers, cafeterias, cutting edge technologies, and staff members for every subject, issue, or potential problem. The government has designed schools as the most expensive way imaginable to educate a child. I could teach social studies to kids in a quarter of the time at a tenth of the cost, and they would learn more sitting in my garage than they would at the local public school. Critics never argue that point, they talk about free and reduced lunches, wrap around services, and extracurricular opportunities. It is an inadvertent admission that their schools are not about educating; they are social agencies which double as jobs programs. Under a decentralized system efficiency and results would take precedent. The most innovative methods would be replicated in a competitive market and substantially drive down the cost to educate. Thirty years ago it would be possible to have a cell phone, a video recorder, a GPS system, and video conferencing capabilities, but you literally would have had to have been a millionaire. Free markets have made each of those affordable to the masses; even my poorest students have them, and on one device no less. Virtually everything else in our lives has been innovated, made better, and made cheaper, except education. This is because there has been a protective government monopoly over the system for 150 years. Poverty is not a barrier to education, that is a myth. Even the world's poorest people have found ways to educate themselves when they are free to do so. The government has interfered with the market's natural tendency to deflate, and has made education far more costly than it should be.

The short answer is I would not replace public schools with anything because they do not need a replacement. It is time we thought about education in a different way. When we think about the vast, entrenched system of buildings, busses, lunches, sports, and strict calendars, it may seem a bit overwhelming to envision an alternative. If it is all you have ever known how do you conceive of a world without it? Education is not different than other economic products. It is subject to the same laws of economics as cell phones are, and can be better, cheaper, and more efficient if we just allow it to.

Works Cited

Chapter 1

"German - A New Surge of Growth -

Immigration...- Classroom Presentation: Teacher

Resources - Library of Congress." *German - A*

New Surge of Growth - Immigration...- Classroom

Presentation | Teacher Resources - Library of

Congress,

www.loc.gov/teachers/classroommaterials/present

ationsandactivities/presentations/immigration/ger

man4.html.

Scafidi, Benjamin Ph.D *"Back to the Staffing Surge."*

EdChoice. Indianapolis, IN. May 2017

"The Nation's Report Card: Trial Urban District

Assessment Reading 2009: District of Columbia

Public Schools (DCPS): Grade 4." *PsycEXTRA*

Dataset, 2010, doi:10.1037/e599542011-001.

U.S. Census Bureau. "Largest Annual Increase in Public School Spending Since 2008." *The United States Census Bureau*, 21 May 2019, www.census.gov/library/stories/2019/05/largest-annual-increase-public-school-spending-since-2008.html.

Public School Student, Staff, and Graduate Counts by State: School Year 2000-01--Ed Tabs: April 2002, nces.ed.gov/pubs2003/snf_report03/.

Chapter 2

Massachusetts Compulsory Attendance Statutes from 1852-1913, www.mhla.org/information/massdocuments/mglhistory.htm.

Wilson, Mitchell. "Cyrus McCormick." *Encyclopædia Britannica*, Encyclopædia Britannica, Inc., www.britannica.com/biography/Cyrus-McCormick

Roser, Max. "Economic Growth." *Our World in Data*, 24 Nov. 2013,

ourworldindata.org/economic-growth.

"Obo." *The Society for the Propagation of the Gospel in Foreign Parts - Atlantic History - Oxford Bibliographies*, 20 Aug. 2019, www.oxfordbibliographies.com/view/document/obo-9780199730414/obo-9780199730414-0067.xml.

Peterson, Robert A. "Education in Colonial America: Robert A. Peterson." *FEE Freeman Article*, Foundation for Economic Education, 1 Sept. 1983, fee.org/articles/education-in-colonial-america/.

Johnson, Claudia Durst. *Daily Life in Colonial New England*. Greenwood Press, 2001

Reich, Jerome R. *Colonial America*. Prentice-Hall, 2001.

West, Edwin G., et al. *Education and the State: a Study in Political Economy*. Liberty Fund, 1994.

Polk, William Roe. *The Birth of America: from before Columbus to the Revolution.* HarperCollins Publishers, 2006.

Chapter 3

Griscom, John. *A Year in Europe: Comprising a Journal of Observations in England, Scotland, Ireland, France, Switzerland, the North of Italy, and Holland. In 1818 and 1819.* Published by Collins & Co. and E. Bliss and E. White, 1823.

Strauss, Gerald. *History of Education Quarterly,* Cambridge Press. Vol. 28, No. 2 (Summer, 1988), pp. 191-206

Records of the Imperial University of France, 19th century. Edinburgh University Library Special Collections. GB 237 COLL-322
Napoleonic Reforms - HistoryWiz Napoleon and the French Revolution,

www.historywiz.com/reforms.htm.

The Revolution, Napoleon, and Education,

www.napoleon-

series.org/research/society/c_education.html.

Staff, HistoryNet. "Battle of Jena: Napoleon's

Double Knock-out Punch." *HistoryNet*, HistoryNet,

23 June 2016, www.historynet.com/battle-of-jena-

napoleons-double-knock-out-punch.htm.

"Addresses to the German Nation/Second

Address." *Addresses to the German

Nation/Second Address - Wikisource, the Free

Online Library*,

en.wikisource.org/wiki/Addresses_to_the_German

_Nation/Second_Address.

Gatto, John Taylor. *The Underground History of

American Education*. Oxford Village Press, 2000.

Russell, Bertrand. *The Impact of Science on

Society*. Routledge, 1994.

Chapter 4

"New England Historical Society." *New England

Historical Society,

www.newenglandhistoricalsociety.com/.

Rothbard, Murray N. *Education, Free &*

Compulsory. Ludwig Von Mises Institute, 1999.

Carleton, David. "Old Deluder Satan Act of 1647."

Old Deluder Satan Act of 1647,

www.mtsu.edu/first-amendment/article/1032/old-

deluder-satan-act-of-1647.

"Constitution of Massachusetts." *Constitution of*

Massachusetts, 1780,

www.nhinet.org/ccs/docs/ma-1780.htm.

Neem, Johann N. *Democracy's Schools: the Rise*

of Public Education in America. John Hopkins

University Press, 2017.

Gordon, Robert J. *The Rise and Fall of American*

Growth: the U.S. Standard of Living since the Civil

War. Princeton University Press, 2017.

West, Edwin G., et al. *Education and the State: a*

Study in Political Economy. Liberty Fund, 1994.

Stowe, C. E., and Samuel Lewis. *The Prussian System of Public Instruction and Its Applicability to the United States*. Truman and Smith, 1836.

Rivington, James. "PROCEEDINGS OF THE BRITISH ACADEMY." *Reform in Great Britain and Germany 1750 - 1850,* www.thebritishacademy.ac.uk/pubs/proc/volumes/pba100.html.

Messerli, Thomas Lloyd., and Horace MANN. *Horace Mann. A Biography*. Alfred A. Knopf, 1972.

Vaughan, Robert. *The Age of Great Cities; or, Modern Civilization Viewed in Its Relation to Intelligence, Morals and Religion*. Jackson, 1843.

Chapter 5

Lepore, Jill. *These Truths: a History of the United States*. W. W. Norton & Company, 2018.

Cova, Antonio de la. *19th Century U.S. Immigration Statistics*, www.latinamericanstudies.org/immigration-statistics.htm.

Beecher, Lyman. *A Plea for the West ... Second Edition.* Cincinnati, 1836.

Mulkern, John R. *The Know Nothing Party in Massachusetts: the Rise and Fall of a People's Movement.* Northeastern Univ. Pr., 1990.

Anbinder, Tyler. *Nativism and Slavery: the Northern Know Nothings and the Politics of the 1850s.* ACLS History E-Book Project, 2005.

Murphy, Robert P. "The Origins of the Public School: Robert P. Murphy." *FEE Freeman Article*, Foundation for Economic Education, 1 July 1998, fee.org/articles/the-origins-of-the-public-school/.

"The Phrenological Journal and Science of Health." *Google Books*, Google, 1839. pg. 380

Tomlinson, Stephen. *Head Masters: Phrenology, Secular Education, and Nineteenth-Century Social Thought*. University of Alabama Press, 2013.

Chapter 6

Katz, Michael S. *A History of Compulsory Education Laws*. Phi Delta Kappa Educational Foundation, 1976.

"Wisconsin v. Yoder." *Legal Information Institute*, Legal Information Institute, www.law.cornell.edu/supremecourt/text/406/205#writing-USSC_CR_0406_0205_ZO.

Attendance.", "Compulsory School. "Compulsory School Attendance." *Encyclopedia of Education*, Encyclopedia.com, 2019, www.encyclopedia.com/social-sciences-and-law/education/education-terms-and-concepts/compulsory-school-attendance.

"Oregon Compulsory Education Laws." *Findlaw*,

21 June 2016, statelaws.findlaw.com/oregon-

law/oregon-compulsory-education-laws.html.

"Pierce v. Society of Sisters." *Legal Information*

Institute, Legal Information Institute,

www.law.cornell.edu/supremecourt/text/268/510#

writing-USSC_CR_0268_0510_ZO.

"State by State." *Coalition for Responsible Home*

Education, 11 Dec. 2014,

www.responsiblehomeschooling.org/policy-

issues/state-by-state/.

Home School Legal Defense Association.

"Homeschooling Advocates since 1983." *HSLDA*,

hslda.org/content/.

Tenenbaum, J.c.c. "Browse Cases." *Legal*

Research Tools from Casetext,

casetext.com/case/knox-v-obrien.

Chapter 7

Cubberley, Ellwood Patterson. *Readings in the History*

of Education: a Collection of Sources and

Readings to Illustrate the Development of

Educational Practice, Theory, and Organization.

Houghton Mifflin Company, 1920.

Michigan State University. "Nearly 1 Million Children

Potentially Misdiagnosed with ADHD."

MSUToday,

msutoday.msu.edu/news/2010/nearly-1-million-

children-potentially-misdiagnosed-with-adhd/.

Matthiessen, Connie. "Why Are so Many College

Students Returning Home?" *Parenting,*

www.greatschools.org/gk/articles/dropping-out-

of-college-record-numbers/.

Chapter 8

Strauss, Valerie. "Analysis | Bill Gates Spent Hundreds

of Millions of Dollars to Improve Teaching. New

Report Says It Was a Bust." *The Washington*

Post, WP Company, 5 Apr. 2019,

www.washingtonpost.com/news/answer-

sheet/wp/2018/06/29/bill-gates-spent-hundreds-

of-millions-of-dollars-to-improve-teaching-new-

report-says-it-was-a-bust/.

Chapter 9

"School Refusal." *Anxiety and Depression Association of*

America, ADAA, adaa.org/living-with-

anxiety/children/school-refusal

STUDENT ASSESSMENTS IN PUBLIC SCHOOLS

NOT STRATEGIC, OFTEN REDUNDANT;

https://www.cgcs.org/cms/lib/DC00001581/Centri

city/Domain/4/Testing%20Report.pdf

Robin Schiltz, et al. "Sexual Abuse by Teachers Is on

the Rise - The Children's Center for Psychiatry,

Delray Beach, FL." *The Children's Center for*

Psychiatry, Psychology, & Related

Services, 29 May 2019,

childrenstreatmentcenter.com/sexual-abuse-teachers/.

American Psychological Association, American

Psychological Association,

www.apa.org/pi/ses/resources/indicator/2013/05/

urban-schools.

"What Makes Urban Schools Different?" *PISA in Focus*,

2013, doi:10.1787/5k46l8w342jc-en.

Lemonis, Marcus (Host). (2016). *The Profit in Cuba.*New

York, NY: CNBC Originals.

Chapter 10

Caplan, Bryan Douglas. *The Case against Education:*

Why the Education System Is a Waste of Time

and Money. Princeton University Press, 2019.

Manzo, Kathleen Kennedy. "The State of Curriculum."

Education Week, 23 Feb. 2019,

www.edweek.org/ew/articles/1999/05/19/36curric

.h18.html.

Gates, Frederick Taylor. *The Country School of to-*

Morrow. General Education Board, 1924.

Mcdaniel, Rhett. "Bloom's Taxonomy." *Vanderbilt University*, Vanderbilt University, 13 Aug. 2018, cft.vanderbilt.edu/guides-sub-pages/blooms-taxonomy/.

Schoology. "SAMR Model: A Practical Guide for EdTech Integration." *Schoology*, www.schoology.com/blog/samr-model-practical-guide-edtech-integration.

Chapter 11

Gatto, John Taylor. *Weapons of Mass Instruction: a Schoolteacher's Journey through the Dark World of Compulsory Schooling*. New Society Publishers, 2017.

Wagner, Tony. *Global Achievement Gap*. Basic Books, 2009.

"Chronic Absenteeism in the Nation's Schools." *Chronic Absenteeism in the Nation's Schools*, www2.ed.gov/datastory/chronicabsenteeism.html

Chapter 12

"The Early Years." *John Taylor Gatto*,

www.johntaylorgatto.com/johns-bio/.

Gatto, John Taylor. *Dumbing Us Down*. New Society

Publishers, 2005.

Community Panel. Personal Interview. May 2019

Shumow, Lee. *Parents' Educational Beliefs:*

Implications for Parent Participation in School

Reforms, 1997.

http://www.adi.org/journal/ss01/chapters/chapter

15-shumow.pdf

Chapter 13

"Search Form." *ISTEP for Families | IDOE*,

www.doe.in.gov/assessment/istep-families.

"New York Education Data Hub." *Nyschooldata*,

www.nyeducationdata.org/.

"Program for International Student Assessment (PISA) -

Mathematics Literacy: Average Scores." *National Center for Education Statistics (NCES) Home Page, a Part of the U.S. Department of Education,* nces.ed.gov/surveys/pisa/pisa2015/pisa2015highlights_5.asp.

"OES News Release." *U.S. Bureau of Labor Statistics*, U.S. Bureau of Labor Statistics, www.bls.gov/oes/.

US Census Bureau. "2017 Public Elementary-Secondary Education Finance Data." *The United States Census Bureau*, 19 Apr. 2019, www.census.gov/data/tables/2017/econ/school-finances/secondary-education-finance.html.

Personal Essay

"Understanding 'Other Health Impairment.'" *Special Education Guide,* www.specialeducationguide.com/disability-profiles/other-health-impairment/.

"Early Academic Training Produces Long-Term Harm."

Psychology Today, Sussex Publishers,

www.psychologytoday.com/us/blog/freedom-

learn/201505/early-academic-training-produces-

long-term-harm.

"A Brief History of Education." *Psychology Today*,

Sussex Publishers,

www.psychologytoday.com/us/blog/freedom-

learn/200808/brief-history-education.

Friedman, Milton, and Rose D. Friedman. *Free to*

Choose: a Personal Statement. A Harvest Book,

2006

Made in the USA
Las Vegas, NV
06 May 2022

48490776R00083